reflections
in the mirror
of time

poems of faith, hope and humor

Rich Houseknecht

To Marge and Fred
with best wishes
for the new millennium

Rich

12-28-99

Published by:
Lifestyles Press
P.O. Box 493
Greensboro, NC 27429

ISBN# 1-58320-006-1

Cover design by Gemini Group
Edited by Henri Forget

To contact author directly please e-mail at:
rich141@juno.com

To my wife, Barbara
To the children: Pam, Ken, Bob, Theresa and Gerry
and those who have joined them in the bond of love
Diana, Mark, Shelly and Chris
To the grandchildren: Danielle, Julia, Alaina,
Caleb, Hayden and Hannah
The great joy is their generosity,
compassion, faith and friendship.
What a great gift they are!

****

Too oft I can not speak aloud
These holy things I hold within
Which move me so and truth uncloud
Of where I'm going and where I've been!

foreword

*O*ne thing that is sure when we look at our lives in review: we are unable to change any of it. What has happened - has happened. Like it or not, history is not flexible. What *is* flexible is how we look at the events and outcome of our lives. We can be kind to ourselves and those with whom we have shared all of those years or we can hold ourselves in the prison of self-recrimination.

One of the ways that I have resolved that conflict in my life has been to write about it in verse. I found that if I did this, the process dug deeply within me and uncovered a sense humility, appreciation, hope, joy or awe that wasn't apparent on first glance. Another way I have dealt with the past has been to plunge into the future as vigorously as I could. There is much satisfaction if one finds worthwhile things to do and not only makes an effort each day to do these things but to do them with sensitivity. That qualifier makes each day's efforts a constant challenge. It is a challenge to be kind and considerate of each person we encounter that day. It is a challenge to show humility. What we accomplish is no more important than how we accomplish it. Throughout this process of day-to-day dedication to living life fully, we must constantly confront the fact that what we have done with our lives heretofore is finished. We can't dwell on those happenings in a negative manner. True, the past is cast in stone but the future, however long that may be, can still be shaped and molded in a hopeful manner.

Time and life go on and we are ever visited by new events, ideas, tasks and reflections. A brother and his wife celebrate their golden wedding anniversary; a letter comes from a cousin that sparks some thought about a grandparent that died in our youth; all the aches and indignities of getting older that lead us to laugh at ourselves and have some fun with words. The reflections in the mirror of time continue with a scope from the most serious to the most frivolous. Just as life does; all different moods and all different emotions: fear and hope, laughter and tears, pain and joy, weakness and strength, death and life, good and bad, we and God. And through it all I keep on writing. *Nulla dies sine linea*; never a day without a word. It is good for the mind. It is good for the soul. It has brought out what I feel and think and hope.

The reflections in this book are more than just a look back at life from the vantage point of the retirement years. They are an effort to find humor, beauty and meaning in life as it now is, at this time and in this place. This work, like life itself, is always a work in progress and will never be finished. It is my way of meeting the challenge of getting older and doing it in a way that is hopeful. I write these things as self-reflection to give me insights that I can return to again and again when the dark parts of the past threaten to lead to despair. What I have written was not done with the intent of presenting it to others except for my family and a few close friends. Now I share these verses with you. Perhaps you will find something that resonates in your experience. Perhaps you will find something in them that will move you. That is my hope.

Rich Houseknecht
8/1/99

table of contents

diamonds of the heart

the chest in the attic

touched and moved

the first miracle

friends, family and other treasures

faith --the lights in the darkness

the lighter side

hope and healing

truths and omens

diamonds
of the
heart

◆◆◆◆◆◆◆

In The Stillness

Are we not inclined to look
Past miracles so near;
A smiling child, a crystal brook,
The friends that give us cheer?

There's miracles around us all
Each hour of each day.
They wait for us to trip and fall
So we will look their way.

Like Naaman do we not resist *
The humble from our ways;
Letting worldly voice persist
To seek and court malaise?

God's gifts are found in stillness
And on humble, gentle lanes;
A walk in winter chillness,
Or the scent of gentle rains.

And in the new born's presence
With wonderment we see,
A reflective, holy essence
Of pure serenity.

The facets of Love's many pearls
Hold nothing shrill nor proud.
They rest in unassuming furls
And seldom speak aloud.

*2 Kings 5: 1-15

Recalling My Grandfather

Memories of long ago, so much beyond recall,
Yet Mother's Dad, his eyes aglow, stands keen above it all.
I was but a mite that's true, and he a giant tall ...
Railroad person through and through, at watch and whistle's call.

I see that day like crystal fair; my Grandpa strong and kind,
With window's light through whitened hair; the smile ... the active mind.
There's much that's vague about that day, but still his presence lingers,
What he wore I could not say, yet see his hard-worked fingers.

Many railroad books he shared with engines steaming strong,
So close my mem'ry's eye is bared, like time was not that long.
He took me on his lap that day, his manner warm and slow,
'Twas like a magic holiday, that day so long ago.

Four sons had he and grand were they, all handsome, strong and true,
Each was made a railroad man ... and each a good man, too!
Each it seemed did suffer much, for life to them was stern,
And though much sadness came to touch, they seldom voiced concern.

One I never heard about, the other three I knew,
One was thought a roustabout, the least among the crew.
Ray's the one who with me starred, my friend was he and good,
He drove the Switcher in the yard, and took us when he could.

He made you feel he really cared, and talked to us at length,
And though he spoke in mildest terms, one saw his inner strength.
He had two children - one a son - who was from Father's mold,
Sadly lost to war, that one, leaving grief untold.

One of the four - Walt was his name - who ran the fastest trains,
A hundred miles per hour claim, when Walt was at the reins.
One day it came like lightning flash, struck down while in the cab,
His color turned a sickly ash, while pain immense did stab!

Would've beaten down a lesser man, but he set the throttle right,
Corrective measures thus began, his second took the flight.
The day was saved and many who, were on the train that day,
Would never know that gallant crew, prevented run-away!

His son named Will I did not know, it seems a shame to say,
It's strange what fam'lies undergo, when ties have gone astray.
I'd bet he was a hero, too; I'd seen it in the others
The depths within from which they drew, the strength that marked his brothers.

Tom it was - the blackest sheep - so thought the haughty prudish,
Some thought him lost in mire deep, and just a bit too crudish.
Common law they said it was, his missus bore the shame,
Of backyard talk and churchy buzz, condemning Tommy's dame.

Now later generations live, for whom that is the norm,
And we for our part do forgive, when some don't quite conform.
But to a lad of five I'd say, Tom didn't seem so bad,
And when he put the gin away, he wasn't such a cad.

They died so young those older ones; we seldom got to know 'em,
But what we learned of Grandpa's sons, was little that would slow 'em!
The four boys weren't the only ones, was also two young misses,
To keep in check those growing sons, e'er keen to see where Sis is.

The sister, Gert, a sweetheart was; a friend to younger kin;
She had a welcome in her smile and cookies in the bin.
Even now her daughters write; I'll see 'em now and then;
We'll chat of days from second sight, and just be kids again.

The sister, Kit, I once called Mom, she's owed my endless thanks,
For bravely raising us with calm, to goodly moral banks.
I think of all the roads they paved, those children and their Dad;
Their lore ... I wished my mem'ry'd saved ... such treasures that I had!

A Wooded Pond At Twilight

Once upon a wooded glen ... sweet and hushed,
The twilight coaxed a healing spirit there,
And soothed the day ... and all its troubles flushed
To vanish in the crisp and fragrant air.

The sky, now fading memory of day,
Had kept its best to show in that sweet hour;
Gold ... pink ... and blue in masterful array;
A silent psalm of praise to silent power.

The pond once blemished healed its wrinkled face,
Now still beneath the setting sylvan sun.
A distant loon met nature's slowing pace,
With one last flight ere soaring grace is done.

Within that mirrored glade, the moment glowed;
Its image true to heaven's gentle hues;
No color lost, no flaw or error showed,
No altered tone an errant brush would choose.

The glory of that pool was not its own,
Though much of beauty did it have to give,
But in reflecting quietly was shown
A greater view it held more sensitive.

I've seen that quiet soul, that humble bent,
That shines with image good and true and bright,
Alive with heaven's hues and wonderment,
A glowing portrait ... pure as still twilight.

Coming To My Lenses

Those ugly glasses gone again, they've gone and lost themselves,
Or maybe carried off aways by some mischievous elves.
Whenever I've a task to do that calls for vision bright,
They've gone to take a walk again; they're just plumb out of sight.

Searchin' for those spectacle's a frus-ter-a-tin' task,
'Cus when I look, my eyes might's well be covered with a mask.
What I need's a miracle to make 'em call to *me*;
A tone, a smell, a sour taste that tells me where they be!

Perhaps I need an animal that's trained to track 'em down,
Instead of chasin' sticks and such - he'd be my eyeball-hound.
Of course he'd have to understand my ways of losing things,
And have the patience to persist through all my blatherings.

I'm sure that if I found him, I'd be so thunderstruck,
He'd surely take his option year and go to try his luck
At someplace where his master had better things in mind,
Than overplaying hide and seek with spectacles to find.

And so I've come to realize such pet will not be found;
That though I search through field and zoo I'll never find that hound;
And still I'll lose and search and lose until the day I die;
Flitting forth from Zed to North like a drunken dragonfly.

It's clear to me there really isn't any good solution,
So now with water, sea and air there's spectacle pollution.
The Lions' Club will meet their goals collecting all the old ones,
If only they will sniff my trails ... especially the cold ones.

The Blue Ridge

There is a place that's heaven-touched like fragrance newly dawned,
With mossy-speckled ancient rock and forest lushly spawned.
Now and then a hidden stream will lead one to a pond,
With lily pads and reed and fern with every shape of frond.
At dusk the scent of ash-smoke comes, adrift from distant camps,
Sweetly there in cool still air, a friend to evening damps.

A swig or two of moonshine helps a little after seven,
To warm a chilly summer's sleep where night-light
comes from heaven.
The whistle sound of distant train beyond all chance to view,
Heralds the foggy dark across the hills of mountain dew.
Hootin', rustlin', twigs a droppin', echoin' through the night,
An angry 'coon a screechin' and a lookin' for a fight.

When night comes to the Blue Ridge scene there isn't man alive
Who wouldn't wonder just a bit what Nature will contrive
A majesty ... A mystery ... a presence in the night ...
Dark and silent ... damp beguilant ... unseen ghostly sprite,
Imagination doesn't sleep in these dark vales and streams,
And long and deep the night disturbs the poor flat-lander's dreams.

The bacon smell surrounds the lodge in early morning fog,
And coffee steams and toast abounds to quell the linger'd grog .
Soon saddled to an easy gait in waken'd morning gleam,
A dozen horses single file o'er switchback trails and stream,
Riders ducking heads below the newly forming branches,
That seem to say 'this road is closed - from here you takes your chances'.

But soon comes quiet mountain lake a home to lone canoe,
The water tanned and smoothly kept a distant mile or two.
Slow driven water mills are seen with sluices many places,
Mist filtered through an arch of trees adorned with fern-shoelaces.
Blue ridge beyond blue ridge and on the ridges seem to go,
'Til lost a foggy distance off in shapeless indigo.

Orchards aged five score and more with knarled and twisted branches,
And roughly crisped darkened bark 'mid coarsely mottled blanches.
One-lane bridges, rutty lanes and whooshing rivers flowin',
Sudden storms with lightning close and thund'rous winds a blowin'.
Toppled trees that speak of storms once visited this wood,
Their upturned roots a musty grave where once they proudly stood.

At end of trail a waterfall with lofty sculpted cliffs,
Sending misted spray aloft in freshly dampened whiffs,
Around are bushy flowered trees and covered hide-a-ways,
With constant buzz of guarding bees that limit stops and stays.
Sweet and damp the essence there of Nature's perfumed juice,
Winds and birds of varied songs fill huddled pine and spruce.

Blue Ridge Mountains, massive land with ancient hills of green,
Land of magic, wondrous places, most I've ever seen!
A place of moonlit valleys and of rock-strewn knobs and hills,
Where yonder smoke that sneaks about reveals the moonshine stills.
Quilts and carvings, walking sticks, log rails and cabins, too,
Friendly folk with banjos strummin' roastin' barbeque.

Take me to the Blue Ridge, boys, oh take me when I die
Right there among the Blue Ridge, boys, between them trees to lie.
Take me to the Blue Ridge, boys, with views that go forever,
There among the Blue Ridge, boys, and let me leave there ... never!
Lay me in the pourin' rain with misty clouds a seepin'
O'er every ridge and hollow where God's beauty is a keepin'!

Late Autumn
A Reflection

In a month the trees will sleep
Waiting for new life to come;
Holding hands against the chill
And darkness of the winter glum.

Those colors now a thinning brown
A parity in death assumed;
The green days long a memory
As branch by branch is empty-roomed.

The blowing hordes of brown and grey
Whisper death in winter's wind;
Each day a shortened gem to grasp
Staunchly held and disciplined.

We live our days of green so quick,
Then autumn comes and paints our souls;
Quickly glimpse life's colors there,
Just before our winter tolls.

Spring ... that new life coming forth ...
From where? From winter white and cold.
From where? From other hues gone brown ...
And other life once drab and old.

John 6: 37-40

Mother

Brilliant in a darkened world,
"Mother" inked below her name --
Knitted meek with kindness purled,
Never would she greatness claim.

As a weak and growing child,
She was there to cultivate
Things of spirit, rich and mild --
Virtues small and virtues great.

Lifetime lessons deeply taught,
Much by work and much by word;
Patient wisdom ne'er forgot --
Clarity where truth is blurred.

When all others turned away,
She was always there with love.
When the demons held their sway,
She brought peace that rose above.

Selfless patron of God's way,
Always did she keep the view
You would come to shine one day,
You would be a dream come true.

Even when you missed the goal,
Never did she rancor show.
Seeing pearls among the coal,
She brought hope to make them glow.

Years go by, her presence looms,
Reverie so sweet and grand.
Rose that ev'ry season blooms,
Beauty given heart and hand.

Whether living or gone on,
She will always special be.
Lovely, loving paragon,
Always was she there for thee.

Hear the echoes of her songs,
Themes that evermore recur
As you wander through life's throngs,
There her mem'ries ever stir.

Remembrance

Eyes cast with gleaming hope from distant shores,
To nation safe from tyrant's whim and pain,
To place where valor raises freedom's reign,
And faces foes a passive world ignores.
Eyes cast where all are free and virtue soars,
Where dignity assures the common gain,
Where rule of law protects each man's domain,
And binding faith in fellow man restores.
This land for whom those many good men fell,
And paid a ransom soaked in tears and red,
Before their years chimes tolled their ending knell,
Commanding us a higher road to tread.
O Liberty, you ask of us to dwell,
In faithful service to those hallowed dead.

the chest
in the
attic

My Father

I never knew my father,
He little knew his son,
Dad wasn't one to bother ...
To play or have much fun.
He seemed to me so serious,
But I just liked to play,
Fun was to me delirious,
His thoughts he would not say.

He left when I was just a boy
Of eight or nine or ten.
Though I regarded him with joy,
He wasn't there again.
It seemed that heaven beckoned more
For him, his home to make;
And empty tales of father-lore
Would boyhood dreams forsake.

I didn't know what "father" meant,
When I became a man.
My resume missed much content
To lead a family clan.
So if my father came today
To see his aged son ...
This to him is what I would say,
"Our friendship's just begun!"

"We've lived our lives alike now,
We're much the same it's true.
We did our best to find out how
A dad was supposed to do.
And if we failed to do it well,
Don't judge us all that bad;
Our scripts with missing chapters tell
There weren't much there 'bout Dad!"

-15-

Once Upon A Yuletide

See the snow ... the flakes ... big as whitened leaves.
The icicles ... like frozen crystal dreams on eaves.
The frosted window ... rimed like some old Currier and Ives ...
Framing into memories the winter scene.
And soon a gentle darkness comes ...
Quiet, soft as cotton ... and by heaven ... so serene.

Christmas Eve!
Beautiful, wonderful Christmas Eve!
Is there a lovelier night in all the year?
Is there?
Snowy, crisp and decorated with Love ...
Christmas Eve!
And look! There's the Christmas tree!
That Christmas tree of youth ... there never will be another like it .
The magic, wondrous Christmas spirit is alive in its branches .
No matter their sparsity ...
Selected and cut by family committee -
Each child has their voice.
A work of art and negotiation ... that tree ...
Into the house it goes with snow still clinging to its boughs ...
Decorated with devotion and memory and the beginnings of ...
... traditions ...
Dad strings the lights, Gerry hangs the first ornament,
Mom does the icicles ...
More than tinsel and lights ... this tree.
Close your eyes and see it!
Every ornament is artistry -
Some made last Tuesday in Grade One.
Some spanning back a generation ... or two ...
Parents' time and grandparents' too ...
Each a cheerful memory to evoke awaiting a family expert
to recall its history.
Later we will keep a vigil at the tree very late into the night ...
With only its lights shining their ... Peace on earth ...
Their warmth penetrating into our hearts ...
We gather for a prayer and Christmas dinner.
We gather for excitement and merriment and joviality
We gather to once again savor that mystic time and joy
That ties us so close back over the years to other times ...
That ties us so close to all those loved ones now gone ...
... And we remember ... there in the flicker of the fireplace.
And now. What are we remembering now? More than a generation later?

-16-

Kids all grown and gone. California, New York, Arizona ...
Some return again ... some can not ...
No one can return to the magic of then ...We can only remember ...
The memories flood forth from some distant, other world ...
Days gone by ... a time ...
a place you wish again your eyes in joy could visit ...
The streets so still ... with distant carolers ...
their songs so known and loved:
O Come All Ye Faithful ... join us in this Silent Night ...
In heart to be your way of life ...
And in the air - crisp but kindly air ...
the sweet and earthy smell of firesides
Where stockings soon will hang ... filled with thoughtfulness ...
... and love.

Our walk to Mass is a parade of seven ...
From tall down to one too small for his snowsuit,
Sitting snug there upon the sled.
The crunching snow ... a sound I've never heard but there.
Soon we pass the living manger scene ...
With Joseph rubbing hands for warmth ...
And Mary-holding her doll-providing a shivered smile as ...
... we walk past.
Here's the church.
How beautiful the Mass - the hymns - the pageantry -
the reverence and love
The story told which never does get old or worn.
The bread of life - born once again within this very time and place.

Now back we walk by houses each adorned with lights ...
The fallen snow has made carpets inches upon inches deep
Still it comes - and greets the children's outstretched tongues and hands.
Crunch - crunch - crunch - what magic in the air!
Soon the sky will clear and moon and stars will sing a silent carol
all their own,
And paint a silver glaze upon the drifts and roofs ...
And places where the road was ...
a few hours ago.
Home again - faces cold and red.
Soon the children are in their red pajamas - feet 'n all -
Toes peeking out holes here and there.
Excitement is worn in smiles and eyes that later will not sleep.
Time now to wind down - time for adults to go to work;
A secret time for kids not to see.
Santa Claus is coming to town!
The children are now in bed ...

Time for Joe to come by with his set of sleigh bells.
Where he got them, I'll never know.
But they are real ... a three-foot string ...
And sooo melodious!
A harmony from an old barn or pawn shop or elderly uncle
or who knows where!
So now the neighborhood dads take turns running between the houses
Shaking the bells!
The message is clear! The message is heard in the dark bedrooms!
Close your eyes!
Santa is coming!

It's almost time for Clark Kent and Lois Lane to become
Santa and His Helpers!
Almost time for the presents to come out of the woodwork!
And some will need tools and time and patience and more patience!
Almost time to go to the secret places where the packages live ...
(Years later it would come to our knowledge that what we thought were
good hiding places had mostly been found out by the kids ...
Parents don't know everything!)

For a long, long time,
The upstairs had been emitting subtle sounds betraying
A clutch of children trying sleep ... but not successfully.
But now ... the subtle sounds are still ... The coast is clear!
A duet of silent voices prays, "Kids! -- Stay in bed!"
Here we come, hiding places!

A building-block structure of packages now grows on the floor
Next to the Christmas tree.
We start now to carefully place the presents under the tree ...
Everything has to be just right!
Nothing misplaced ... everything just so!
Then there's the stocking stuffers ... or we should say overstuffers ...
'Cuz some of the stuff spills out onto the mantle ...
Finally ... the frenzy is over ... we sit there soaking it all in ...
Then, after a time ... it hits us ... Santa has come and gone!
We look at each other ... dead tired ... but satisfied and happy ...

A line has been crossed now ...
Christmas Eve has become Christmas!
It is very late ...
And quiet and love settle upon that scene we will never see again ...
The tree ... the packages ... the tricycles ... the doll too big to wrap ...
the lights ...
And all the saving and working and planning and wrapping and hiding ...

Quietly sing their own carol - that says it was all worth it ...
The trials of a family -
The toil - the struggles - the uncertainties - all of it!
Was worth it!
Was it ever!

It will never happen again ...
Except in our most cherished memories ...
And what precious memories they are!
A family has been born and lives!
A Savior has been born and lives!
Merry Christmas!
God is with us!

A Lad At Bedtime

When I, a boy of nine or ten
Went off to bed, to dark and dreams;
I counted shadows in my den
That moved as slaves to headlight beams.
I heard the chugging steam trains, too
Sing songs with sadly rhythmic moans;
Their click, click, click; their whoo, whoo, whoooo ...
Set schemes of fancy with their tones.

A life apart and far away,
A lad envisions tales untold;
Of pictures from some distant day,
Of far-off lands of green and gold.
Those magic nights of long ago
Resound their fancy in my mind,
Of shadowed walls and whistle's blow
From distant days left far behind.

The Penny Post Card

Those simpler times of long ago transmit
A message through the years; a penny's post;
A lonesome boy at camp; his mighty boast
Of scaling all the heights held requisite.
In pencil faint with time and course of writ,
He tells how solidly he is engrossed;
But midst the lines his sadness is foremost;
A childish state he never would admit.
A boy will write his Mom and bravely show
He's tough ... and maybe more than all the rest;
And then he signs it ... "Love" ... and she will know
That in his heart to him she is the best.
Those years and she will pass away although,
Not once will he forget her gentleness.

Tempus Fugit

My mother said short while ago,
"Don't wish your life away.
You'll see time tends to quickly go,
It has the briefest stay."

I'm thirteen now and wonderin' much,
How long it's gonna be,
Before I'll stay out late and such,
Before I'm truly free.

Been wishin' I could drive the car,
And get the stuff I need,
This growin' up, it seems so far,
It never will proceed.

Now forty-two and holdin' fast,
To kids and work and house;
My life is like a simulcast,
With family and spouse.

I wonder when we'll see that day,
When we will be retired,
And habitate that getaway,
For which we've much perspired?

Now sixty-six and goin' strong,
Been thinkin' 'bout my prime.
When it was, it said, "So long!"?
What happened to the time?

That boy thirteen or forty-two,
Sure didn't know the score,
That gettin' old like Grampa Lou,
Weren't such a lengthy chore!

The shortest space is not you see,
The straight line 'tween two points;
But rather twixt impatient teen,
And achin' in the joints!

So Mama, if you're listenin',
You surely had it right,
The time that follows Christenin'
Is really most finite.

The Tourist Home

Oh the house next door was a great old place,
With a tourist sign and a smiling face.
We were kids wide-eyed as we peeked at night,
Seeing life and love in the shadowed light.
There were lots of guests there that came and went,
And a few or so that were negligent
Left the shades unpulled with their clothing gone,
And we learned too much from the goings-on!

In those days of old, 'twas a different way
Parents taught their kids 'bout the rules risque,
And so boys learnt much with their race track mind;
Of anatomy taught through an open blind.
Now the tourists came and the tourists went,
And it seemed that most had a modest bent,
But the few who didn't hold that view
Educated me and my brother too!

Now it weren't as if it obsessed us two,
Or aroused in us even slightest clue
Of the things that make the world go 'round;
Didn't even make our wee hearts pound.
It was just some new ground to explore,
That made us look to the scene next door;
Like a frog or a wart or jack-knife blade,
Or a boondoggle rope that was clever-made.

"Boys are boys" or so the saying goes,
And they'll do such things long as water flows;
Like a lot of things a kid won't tell,
Fearing parents' wrath and the heat of hell.
Now I look back to those days of old,
And I see two boys sometimes fresh and bold,
But then mostly what the memory brings
Are bats and balls and meanderings.

Little came of the spying in the night,
And we grew up rejecting wrong from right;
And I'd have to say to be honest, true,
That the tube has more in a space or two,
Than we ever saw with our glass-pressed eyes;
Than we'd ever draw as the next-door spies!
And the things kids do to their own chagrin,
Next to TV fare are a minor sin!

To My Grandchild

My dear one, I've lived many years of this life,
And there's some things I've come to see clear;
One of them is that through all of this strife,
One can come to reflect with a tear ...

And think of the joy he'd have made of it all,
If only he'd set his sights higher,
The pain never felt - the good of his call,
Because of his lofty aspire.

So sing, Precious One, while the song's still within,
Give it all with your heart and your hand;
Reach for the stars, be the noblest of kin,
And make of yourself something grand.

Never to wend the road comfort descends,
Rise and seek every challenge of mind,
Embracing the heights that each virtue ascends,
Be ye thoughtful and patient and kind.

Let not remorse even echo in thee,
Because you did less than you could have;
But make your life treasures of pure charity,
Devoid of "if only I would have ..."

Romans 12: 9-21

touched
and
moved

Touched And Moved

See it in the plaintive face and the native mother's eyes;
See it in each newfound place that's touched by twilight skies;
Find it in the tropic breeze, and the black-sand breaker's roar;
Hear the singing in the trees, and calypso by the shore.

Faces smiling every tongue, from every shape and hue;
Cultures hidden deep among the palms and briny blue.
Forests blessed by many rains, with life one seldom sees;
Distant mountains, rocky plains with richly flowered leas.

Magic days and restful dreams with lullabies that play
A shushing aire of ocean streams 'til dawn reclaims the day.
Whooshing by at twenty knots with white caps flying high;
Blue on blue, those wavy spots run fast to meet the sky!

A gull flies here ... a gull flies there; one wonders where they nest;
Stretched out ... the sea is everywhere, without a place to rest;
The sky is bright and awesome vast, to frame the running tide,
And when the night surrounds the mast, a million stars abide!

A thread of bonding day by day, pulls life from every sphere,
To weave each heart a place to play ... in beauty ... hope ... and cheer!
At sea ... there is a simple song ... yet beautiful to know;
It's sung where time and space belong to heaven's endless glow!

Aboard *Norwegian Dynasty*
March 18, 1999

Nightspell

That field of diamonds eons wide,
I've gazed there oft in awe.
Timeless scope ... eternal tide;
Brought low by what I saw.
Reflecting as I gazed upon
That ever changeless scene;
Close that soul of Macedon,
Within this view pristine.

Socrates and Euclid there,
Joined in silent spell.
What inspiration as they stare?
What great thoughts caused to dwell?
And there is Paul on dusty road,
In distant lands to teach,
Of love and truth and God's abode
Beckoning our reach.

At war -- sad soldier's eyes rise up,
To meet this scene of peace,
While death and sadness are his cup,
And woes that do not cease.
Once Magi knew and viewed this night,
In following their star;
To reach the holy manger's Light
With gifts brought from afar.

Heaven's there for great and small
Though most disdain the time,
To sense the awe, to heed its call,
And rest in thought sublime.
God, it seems, speaks quiet ways,
His gifts for weak and strong,
Ne'r passing even smallest Soul,
Amidst the greatest throng.

Kings and prophets ... masters great,
No closer to those stars;
Rich men have no special gate,
To Virgo or to mars.
Maybe what we'll find someday,
In leaving here alone;
That countless like those stars' array,
Are brothers never known.

Alone In The Early Morning

The next time you walk early in the morning ...
When you are alone and the beauty of the breaking day has started ...
Look around you with all of your senses
and let it capture you!

It is early morning ... walking ... I encounter no one
as I walk through the wooded park.
Then there is a clearing ...
Light is just now beginning to fill the sky with color.
The texture and variety of color about me has a special golden radiance.
It is dynamic, harmonious ... silent, almost like a palpable presence.
I reflect ...
when we love someone we seem compelled to give them something,
something of ourself.
It must be like that with God, too.
It occurs to me as I look up at the beautiful clouds and sky
and the misty, shimmering rays that are piercing the tree tops ...
Here is a picture that only God can paint ...
And it is being given to me.
It is at this time and in this place
a magnificent painting by God *just for me.*
It must be so ... no one else is here.
I haven't seen a soul in the past half-hour ...
there is no one else in sight.
At this place and this time ... it must be for me alone.
When we love someone, we feel compelled to give them something.
God is speaking as only He can,
"Here is a painting I have created just for you.
Good Morning. I will light your day!"

The Night And The Sea

The warm wind caresses each furl of my being,
And freshens each breath that I take,
I stand here alone ... not a soul to my seeing,
Below ... churning ... the undulant wake.

What creatures abound this ebony deep,
Or lost treasures of ages gone by?
An awesome infinity sealing their keep,
'Neath the eyes of an unending sky.

The wind ... a full measure greater than breeze,
A mite less than the strength of a gale,
A will of its own, going where it will please,
Setting challenge to tiller and sail.

The waves loosely tethered in feathery foam,
Always moving to yonder then gone.
While the clouds nudged by moonlight happily roam,
In search of some distant fair dawn.

A magical place is this sea and these waves,
And this spray and these stars and these clouds.
Here I would stay in these wondrous enclaves,
Touched by their gossamer shrouds.

Deep in my being a concert is playing,
Attuned to this tropical night,
A spiritual flight of harmonic arraying,
A chorus of soul-filled delight.

I sense in this night a kind hand creating,
This planet we mortals call home,
A masterpiece played with sublime orchestrating,
Of stars and of wind and of foam.

A Brief Passing

Pass we here briefly; a limited stay;
Each of us comes from a different way.
A smile each ... a story ... a raised glass of wine;
Uniqueness forthcoming to yours and to mine.

A sharing ... a respite ... in life's long refrain;
A pause to take rest, and to count every gain;
To forget for a moment the rain and the dark;
And breathe joy anew ere we each disembark.

Soon we'll be off to the four compass points;
To familiar venues that each life appoints;
Memory's pictures left playing their games,
Of dimly lit vistas and forgotten names.

But somewhere within us the jade will still gleam,
Of a time we once-strangers shared in a dream;
Of lands we once walked and seas we once sailed,
And friends we once met, and warm days regaled!

Strangers are given a path theirs alone;
Now good and easy ... now hard as stone.
We walk among strangers for just a short while,
The stranger soon lost in the warmth of a smile.

The time passes quickly; we wish each adieu;
Sad that we'll never again rendezvous;
Sad in the bidding "goodbye" and "farewell";
But glad for the album of memories we'll tell.

Aboard *Norwegian Dynasty*
March 16, 1999

The Ever-Present Wind

We hear your loud clamor as evening grows cold,
With the rattling of windows and doors;
Carrying the white stuff with strength ever so bold,
Tending keenly your wintery chores.

We feel your soft touch on a warm summer's day,
Giving voice to the spruce and the pine;
Teasing the willow to dance and to play,
Stirring hordes of Pond's crystals to shine.

Heard in the distance - a rumble off there
An awakening awesome dark might,
Foreboding the skies ... compel us to stare,
At the frightening clouds in full flight.

Your travels are surely an everywhere show,
From mountain to mountainous sea;
You've been there before, wherever we go,
In valley or rippling lea.

You comfort and cool us when summer's so hot
That it taunts us in catching our breath,
No doubt you'll be blessing our burial plot,
As you mournfully wail at our death.

"And my aim in life is to make as many good pictures and drawings as I can and as well as I can. Then, at the end of my life, I hope simply to pass away while looking back with love and wistfulness, thinking, 'Oh, the pictures I might of made!' But this, mind you does not preclude doing what is possible."

***

"... To leave to mankind "some memento in the form of drawings or paintings - not made to please any particular movement; but to express a sincere human feeling."

Vincent Van Gogh (1855 - 1890)

Van Gogh

Reading the story of Van Gogh,
Once quickly, thence repeated slow,
An image shone of one so great,
Gifted ... giving ... in tortured state.
The reflection made me stop and see
How I had missed reality.
Too inward I ... too fleet of thought,
To see the message that I ought.
To learn another's deepest view,
What I alone could ne'er pursue,
And find a wealth of wisdom there,
With spirit raised beyond self care.
From them we find a higher realm,
Where life is borne by truer helm,
Where humbly one reflects in awe,
The beauty shared by what they saw.
Return we now with different view,
To see what treasures we eschew ...
The painting passed with briefest look,
The song dismissed -- the unread book,
The half-heard tale the child would tell,
The garden walked without a smell.
Then stunned ... one day their gift we'll meet,
That opens visions at our feet;
That raises hearts to miles above;
A glimpse revealed of God's own love.

Wee Brooklet

Baptizer of the heart and soul and land;
Elixir of a hope and nation grand;
Sweet music to the lyric of our lives;
Sweet everything an awesome God contrives!

Wee brooklet in the highest mountain clime;
Iced cold ... the wind a knife and blowing white;
The labored stream amid its icy rime,
Goes forth to find a place to warm its flight.
Soon other waters meet its destined path,
And in their journey form a mounting strength;
And creatures come to taste its frothing lath;
And forests seek its gift of life and length.

No easy path, no straight geometry;
At times it leaps from heights to crash and spray,
Then gaining mass and pulled by distant sea,
Once creeping brook now thunders through the day!
Down ... down ... and down ... it blurs the lovely scene,
The smashing sinew sets direct its route;
No fledgling wisp, but screaming forth its mien;
Crazed juggernaut hellbent in chasm chute!

A force all nature heeds with careful note;
The mighty flood speeds on to serve a world
Of needs and hunger wide and thirsts remote,
To give its power life in fields up curled.
Swift course, it yields to hills and checkered plain,
Its placid face now hiding swollen might;
Lifeblood or flood of rage or fields of grain;
Wee brooklet states which chapter it will write.

Its work soon done it gently meets the sea,
To find its place in other life and lore;
To find the storm or find tranquility;
To find new friends in deep or distance shore.
Wee brooklet you've beheld and seen much life;
Tell of the beauty that was always yours;
We've walked your banks and seen in peace and strife
Your rocky courts, the niche swift might secures ...

In rushing falls; in still and frigid air;
On sun-baked sands; on quiet moonlit sea;
In raging storm; in wheat fields gold and fair;
In periled calls or laughing children's glee;
Bereft we'd be without your charm and flight;
Without your waterfall or rushing flood;
Without your field of grain or surging might;
Without your sandy shore or teeming mud.

Wee brooklet, shape our fields and give us life!
With awe we see you in your many ways;
Your countenance, your boundless gifts so rife,
The beauty, hope and joy brought to our days!
Sustainer of the very life of earth;
O pure and clear enabler of it all;
You power, feed and beautify the dearth!
O wee brooklet ... how mighty is your call!

Baptizer of the heart and soul and land;
Elixir of a hope and nation grand;
Sweet music to the lyric of our lives;
Sweet everything an awesome God contrives!

You Taught Me, Friend

Dedicated To
All Who Have Taught Us

You taught me, friend, and I am ever in your debt;
Your gifts are gifts I know I never will forget;
In weakest times, you searched and found my inner strength;
You saw my soul and took full measure of its length;
You saw my goodness, that most others failed to see;
You saw my future, when it was black and grim to me ...
You taught me, friend.

You challenged me and made me reach for lofty stars,
For other worlds and fervent dreams that held no bars,
You took the time and made me see my utter worth,
You showed me truth that kept my feet upon the earth.
When I was wrong, you showed your kind and gentle ways;
When days were long, your smiles erased the gloom and haze ...
You taught me, friend.

I went my way ... but gave you little thanks or praise;
Though much I'd gained from all your blessed sunshine days;
Life, love and growth, were where your lessons steered me to;
Hard work and truth, your bright examples shining through.
Where e'er you be, I will reflect and I will pray
In thanks for you ... your guiding words ... your loving way ...
You taught me, friend ...
And I will be forever changed.

Heaven's Child

The purest soul peered into this world
And found it wanting ...
Chose heaven ...
And remained with God ...

And looking upward ...
The earth cried.
A young father and mother mourned ...
And prayed ...
And tried to understand
A wisdom beyond mortality ...

And this purest child
Waits in heaven ...
And one day
Before another lifetime,
In the brilliance of her Light,
She will kiss them both
And love them,
As they have never known love before ...
And it will be ...
Forever.

A Psalm For Easter

God, you have created everything we sense or know in any way!
From the universe with all its galaxies - to life rising to humanity.
From the complexities of time, space and substance
To the Invisible power of emotions and thought and especially love.

You are -- beyond time -- beyond understanding
-- beyond all created things!
You, O God, are supreme above everything!

God, you created us each with a free will.
Free to love You or not - as we choose.
Free to do good and free to do evil.
And too often we have chosen evil.
But You, O God, out of love, have given us a way to overcome evil -
To save our lives -- in the spiritual sense; the eternal sense.
You, Yourself, came and lived among people as a man.

You, Jesus, came to our world - to teach us - to lead us -
to show us miracles!
You came to show us Who God, Our Creator, is -
and what He wants from each of us.
You called God, "Father." You said we should also call Him,
"Father."
You showed us by Your life on earth that as your servant, John said,
"God Is Love."
You, the One God of all power are the source of all love!

Then, as the ultimate act of Your love for us -
You died in a human sense on the cross -
You accomplished the task of overcoming death for all people through
Your suffering.
You have enabled us to experience spiritual eternity - beyond temporal life.
You conquered death by rising from the grave!
By Your resurection you have gained for each of us eternal life !
- a share in the God life - Forever.
That's what Easter is about, isn't it!
******

And so we celebrate Easter above all other events.
Above all other days.
Not in a distant - third person - way, Lord.
But in a highly personal desire to live.
Not just now, not just today, but Forever!
We thank you, Lord, and we praise You!

John 3: 16

The Homeless Shelter

This quiet night ... the cold mist falls,
A hundred homeless souls are here,
Fed and warmed in the Shelter's walls,
Each one cared for, each one dear.

Warmth and kindness sorely needed,
From the cold, wet, heartless night,
The Lord's sad voice quietly heeded,
For the hundred huddled tight.

"Here's a sick man, his vomit red!"
"See that head of gray."
"Give that girl those shoes." he said,
"Let that sick man stay."

The night moves on ... the clamor stilled,
The hundred dream and groan,
The Shelter's beds now all are filled,
The lonely no longer alone.

Thank God for such a place as this,
For warmth and smiles and cheer,
Though much these days has gone amiss,
There's a hopeful spirit here.

A Prayer At the Shelter

O Lord of all of the Universe, you knew what it was like
to be without a place of your own to rest.
We ask your blessing on each person here tonight so that
While they are without a place of their own to rest,
They may be comforted by the care and concern of those they meet;
And may find a path that will lead them from these trials
To a place of shelter and warmth and love.
In Jesus' name ... Amen.

Matthew 8: 19-20

Crosses Of Stone

The muffled drums ... rolling ... a sad steady beat,
Slow cadence of ages ... life now complete.
The piper intones a hero's refrain
Calling our eyes to the field where they're lain.
See them and count them as far as you see,
See and remember their still sanctity ...
O crosses of stone there ... those crosses of stone,
Debt so profound owed those crosses of stone!
There's many a hero there of this great land,
Many a legend from sea and from sand,
Many a schoolboy those actions once played,
Many a prayer a sad mother prayed.
Many a battle with so many dead,
Many a river that turned bloody red.
There's legions of ghosts who will ne'er be known,
Whose short lives are marked with crosses of stone.
They fell on the sands of Normandy's shores,
Laid in their blood by their bomber's bay doors,
Places with names like Inchon and Pleiku,
Iwo and Khe Sahn and Mogadishu.
Ranks growing larger as time passes on,
Armies of new heroes join those who are gone.
Lo there's many a tyrant - and many a fool,
Who'd enslave and oppress as their way of rule,
There's many a lesson the world never learns,
And bridges of wisdom that ignorance burns.
It was ever thus and seems always will,
The world will find new ways to maim and to kill,
New ways to impoverish the weak and the young,
New ways to trample a color or tongue,

New ways to ignore the good of restraint,
New ways of pretending evil is quaint.
Heroes will be needed throughout this great land,
To meet the new evils that come and demand
Wisdom and duty and courage in strife,
Giving and sacrifice - even one's life.
Many a schoolboy those actions will play,
Many a prayer sad mother will pray.
Many a debt will be laid in the book,
Loss freely taken and pleasures forsook,
Legions of new ghosts will never be known,
Giving their lives up for crosses of stone.
The muffled drums ... rolling ... a sad steady beat,
Slow cadence of ages ... life now complete.
The piper intones a hero's refrain,
Calling our eyes to the field where they're lain.
See them and count them as far as you see,
See and remember their still sanctity ...
O crosses of stone there ... those crosses of stone,
Debt so profound owed those crosses of stone.

Creation

Fifteen or twenty billion years ago in the void of nothingness
something happened!
Billions of years old, now immense in size to our scope
there was a beginning.
They say it came from an infinitesimally small place.
A location in a vast nothingness.
They call it the "big bang" -- all of what we know beginning in a point.
What shall we call it?
Some call it the first cause - some call it the force - some call it *creation!*
A point of what? A point of everything? CREATION!
In space and time - CREATION!
Were there space and time before this cosmic beginning?
Did it occur outside of time? Outside of space? Outside of mass?
Outside our understanding?
What was there in the nothingness before creation? What started it?
And what of the *Creator ?*
When I was a child the awesomeness of these thoughts frightened me.
Still it has me in awe.
That kernel of reality. That kernel of what there was and now is.
Was all that has come since ... there ... in some form of seed?
Call it the CREATION SEED. Call it the CREATION KERNEL.
From within that kernel came
electrons and atoms and worlds and stars and galaxies ...
Galaxies by the billions! Perhaps even billions of billions!
Each with billions of stars!
Matter and energy. Energy and matter.
Different forms of the same thing.
From that infinitesimally small kernel came IMMENSITY!
And most important to us; from that kernel came *life.*
The life multiplied into a variety of forms and species.
The life came as protozoa and microbes and insects and

fish and animals.

The life came as moss and trees and flowers and fruit and grain.

And the life brought fragrance and beauty and sustenance to itself.

And in time came man!

MAN !

And the totality of all life brought inspiration to man.

From man's life sprang forth thought.

Was there contained within that kernel of creation absolute truth?

Some of it or all of it? All there is to know or some of it?

Man ponders. Only some of what he calls truth does he know.

But much of it he can only speculate about and ponder and guess at.

We observe. Some with great brilliance and power of inference.

We postulate.

We test our assumptions.

Logic and reason are our tools.

We progress in understanding but are awestruck
by the sheer magnitude of creation.

From man's life sprang forth curiosity and emotion and
passion and love.

From man's life sprang forth a dichotomy between
solitude and community.

And man questioned where he came from and where he was going.

Are there others? Are we alone in this cosmic universe ...

... that came from that explosive kernel?

Are we here for a purpose? How do we discern that purpose?

And man lives on a sphere where constantly there are reminders of his
pitiful ...

... smallness ...

Man's smallness next to oceans, continents, deserts, mountains,

Earthquakes with their tsunamis, volcanoes, hurricanes,
meteors and comets.

Man's smallness next to the tiny living entities that bring
death and disease ...

and are only partially understood.
Man contemplates his smallness next to life itself ...
next to IMMENSITY!
A continuum of creation to the present.
Sometimes placid, sometimes violent.
Always IMMENSE!
Is there direction in its past? In its future? In where it is heading?
Creation. Immensity.
Always awesome!
An order and beauty and power and magnificence that
reverberates and reveals
... in myriad ways
a Shaping Hand behind it!
... in the thundering quietness of the heavens and
the pulsing we call life.
... in the unseen reality of the invisible ...
thought, reflection, feelings, passion,
and love.
In the unquenchable internal quest to find completeness and communion
with the Creator,
Early man humbled himself before the great IMMENSITY.
Before such magnitude he thought that creation was
created by many gods.
But in time he came to acknowledge one grand
Creator.
And he called the Creator ...
GOD!
And then, in time he made himself known to our tiny part of the cosmos
... God, in a personal revelation of His presence ...
... came forth.
And as we know ourselves to be persons ... God revealed Himself as a
person.
"I am Who is!"
The relationship between God and man becomes a

covenant given by God to man.
And in our humility and insignificance we are given
guidance and hope and love.
And, then again, in time God revealed Himself ...
... in the form of a man ...
... a humble man named ...
Jesus.
And Jesus told the men of his day that when they saw him,
they saw the Father,
And that He was with the Father before men came to be ...
And to us the cosmos was no longer something to be feared.
... And God ...
the same God who has created all that was in that kernel of creation ...
shows us that He is the personification of love ...
... for out of love He has given us human life.
... and out of that love He promises to us His greatest gift ...
... eternal life ...

John 1:1-14

Daybreak!

The morning's crisp-aired essence,
Drawn deep within the breast;
A peaceful inner presence,
Sees all that is the best.

A cormorant comes fishing,
And the flowers lean to sun;
Ending trails of wishing,
As new life is begun!

Thanksgiving to this dew-filled green,
That remnant from the dawn;
The morning sounds; the beauty seen,
When darkest night is gone.

Come spirit of the sunlight,
Come warm the breeze and heart.
Come soul of pure and rich delight,
Come find our better part.

the
first miracle

۞ ۞ ۞ ۞ ۞ ۞ ۞ ۞ ۞

Love

Love is forever,
Exceeding our time,
Beyond our understanding.

Barbara, My Love

One of a kind, her smile and heart,
Her style and mind are always smart,
Though humble, she is ably versed.
Ne'er friend nor stranger ever cursed,
Much faith and trust does she impart
She's just the best your day to start.
With hope and love her quiet art,
Her family always comes in first!
One of a kind!

She'll sometimes horse put after cart,
Yet has a sureness to impart,
Many hurt feelings she has nursed
And once or twice a bubble burst,
But, to the end, she's my sweetheart!
One of a kind!

Nowadays it's hard to find,
A friend that's good and tough and kind,
That makes your day as well as meals
And knows most times just how it feels
To smile and fret and hope and love.
With others' needs placed e'er above
What she would much prefer to do,
She's ever doing things to please ...
We know ... we smile ... we say that she's
One of a kind!

Waning

Years past was such a passion and a pledge,
A future sure of love and faith and hope,
That could with any blight or problem cope,
Ne'er opting for a principle to hedge.
Was loyalty no outside force could wedge,
No person, thing, event bring cause to mope,
Nor cause to change and follow lesser scope.
No hint of scandal was there to allege.
Then time and selfless passion seemed to fade,
In increments each went in their own way,
And purpose waned amid those changes made,
Their lives awash in self and worn cliche.
No outside world to which this loss is laid,
Just gone in little droplets day by day.

True love can aging thrive ... it need not wane,
Like wine its bouquet sweet with passing time,
Its golden song returned in words sublime,
Its selfless dignity once more to reign.
What mystic path that once more sings that strain,
That causes hearts to pound and hopes to climb,
That finds the treasures lost and warms the rime,
That kisses kindness much and heals the pain?
No magic spell this spirit to renew,
Though effort will be needed in the plight,
Patience, trust and cheerfulness will much do,
To start the song and help to set things right.
No pride or angry grudges to accrue,
Just smiles and kindly gestures day and night!

Sapphire Years
45 years of love

Sapphire years are a sparkling blue,
Facets of a lifelong love;
Sapphire years have an ageless hue,
A gift from the Lord above.

The joys and tears -- we began with them
Then a million more were there ...
Trials and fears -- like the rays in the gem
Escaped in the love-filled air.

The facets grew as the years passed by
The hues became deep and wise;
Each was sensed by a keener eye
Like shades in the twilight skies.

Now in a quiet moment or two,
As if touched by an Unseen Hand;
We know what it is that brought us through
To fulfill and to understand ...

Like countless beams in the blue gemstone,
Or the rays through the graying hair;
Our days are a gift where the sun has shone
With our gleaming dreams made fair.

We couldn't know what the years would bring
But we shared our faith and love ...
I thank you, Love, for the song you sing,
It fits my hopes like a glove.

So when e'er you wear your deep blue stone,
Keep in mind these sparkling years ...
The kids, the times that were ours alone,
And hearts full of souvenirs.

Love's Time

Have you the time?
The time for what?
To listen that is all.
For you, I hope I always do ...

Have you the time?
The time for what?
To live, another life or two.
I do ... if it's with you ...

Have you the time?
The time for what?
Eternity to pass through.
O yes ... if it's with you,
I pray I do!

Nature's Junction

Meet me at nature's junction,
At the corner of soul and heart;
In Peace, with no worldly function,
Reach for your spirit's part.

Meet me where flocks soar in the air;
Where Love is always new;
Meet me by the calming waters there,
Just Peace ... and me ... and you.

The Rings Of Love

Your rings have no start, no visible ends,
Symbol of lasting and most cherished friends.
The joy in the eyes, the smiles from the heart,
Souls' inner beauty, with love to impart.
With friends and well-wishers glasses held high,
Some active and dancing, some not so spry,
All celebrating these wonderful two,
This day of the old, the borrowed and blue!

Another with ring is happy to share,
A morsel of wisdom ... some truth to declare ...
Marriage is mystic ... but simple in ways,
Not a lot different from grandfather's days.
Marriage is holy with vows before God,
Love freely given, consensual nod.
Though the focus of marriage stresses the *two*,
It's the *one* and the *one* that makes vows come true!

After the banquet and after the wine,
Life gives us its challenge, tough or benign,
Each must give much and often give in,
Each must be patient with lots of thick skin!
Forgiving and giving ... these are the key,
To build and to strengthen true amity.
There is no assurance how life will ensue,
But much will you gain when honest and true!

Falling in love is a neat little phrase,
But not for the long term and rent never pays ...
Most things that fall will meet a quick stop,
Most things that fall will require a mop!
It takes lots of effort to make marriage work,
Kindness and prayer are nothing to shirk,
Sad times and good times and times in between,
Times overwhelming and times all serene!

The effort it takes to make it work well
Will return o'er and o'er and joyfully dwell
In hearts of those willing to work at their love
And call for light daily from Jesus above!
Your rings have no start, no visible ends,
Symbol of lasting and most cherished friends.
The joy in your eyes, the smiles from your heart,
Will keep your love fresh as it was at the start!

John 2: 1-11

Toasting The Golden Years

(For Ralph and Agnes)

I was there that magic day
When you each replied "I do."
But who could know the winding way
Life's path would take you through?
Some good; some bad; some in between
Has surely come your way.
Some guidance from a Hand unseen
When God seemed far away.

To live as one for fifty years
Takes steady, patient heart.
With joys and laughs and pains and fears
You've wisdom to impart.
Some would ask you how it was
You made the grade so well.
Some would say it was because
You had a song to tell.

Your song is written in the sons
Who carry on your name;
And in the goodness of your girls
And how you've played life's game.
Good friends abound your many years
And make your candle bright;
Their lives surround you now with cheers
To celebrate this night!

For fifty years you've made their days
A sweeter song for them.
For fifty years you've shaped their ways
To them, you are a gem.
And may I say, as good men can
I'm proud that I was there
And proud the fifty years of span
Are not too much for wear.

So here's to years aplenty more,
Before you take your leave
May all the best be yet in store
With little left to grieve.
So here's a toast as friend and kin,
We wish you evermore,
That God's good favor rest within
Your every Golden pore.

Forgiveness

To forgive you from the heart,
And never once be proud,
Each day with prayer start,
Diminishing each cloud.

Never take you, Dear, to task,
Raised voice a whisper be.
Rash judgment never mask
The way I cherish thee.

To restrain my acid tongue,
That causes hurt and pain.
Rather that my song be sung
With kindness as its strain.

To let patience be the art,
Like oil upon the sea,
Forgiving from the heart,
As I would want to be.

Luke 6: 37-38

Ode To My Wife And Friend

If you should die before I'm gone,
I'll search and search and yearn and long
To find your sweet face ... eyes so deep;
With kindness, love and warmth to keep
Me strong amid the awful pain,
And lift my eyes to hope again.

I'll challenge failing mind to bring
Old memories to rise and sing,
Of times and places that we shared,
The special way in which we cared;
Of family and friends so true,
T'would ne'er have been except for you.

And you'll be there when I'm alone,
Walking where your light has shown,
Remembrances a glowing ember,
Vestige of a soul so tender.
But alas ... with passing days I'll rue,
That when death came ... it first was you.

Skipping Stones

Skipping stones across the sea,
Skipping lightly, skipping free,
Smiling sweetly there with me,
Sharing in my gaiety.
Walking beaches in the sand,
Walking slowly, hand in hand,
Blending dreams we'd never planned,
Mending ways, to understand.
Strolling with you side by side,
Footsteps washed by time and tide.

Now you're gone and I'm alone,
Sandy dreams have turned to stone,
The gaiety that love had known,
Gone to where despair is sown.
Now I feel the icy grain
Of cold and empty sands of pain.
Now I walk in waves of rain,
Where love is lost and hope is vain.
Gone the strolling side by side
Footsteps lost to time and tide.

Alone without a hand to hold,
The sea is dark ... the waters cold.
The days are long and empty souled,
Skipping heart now pierced and old.
Those happy, skipping days now end
Heaven's beaches you now wend;
Catch the stones I skip and send,
Hold them with my dreams, my friend.
Keep them with you ... by your side
Bless and warm the time and tide.

Then I'll see you in the sky,
In the white clouds dancing by,
In the song birds soaring high,
In that Presence ever nigh.
I will feel you close to me,
Warming breezes by the sea,
Touching forests ... tree by tree,
Strolling toward eternity.
Soul mates ever side by side
Skipping over time and tide!

A Ship Came Searching

A ship sailed into port one day
And searched to find a friendly hand
To tie its line upon the quay
And welcome it upon the land.
The ship was filled with love and hope,
Though scarred and torn by countless reefs ...
Its log a lush kaleidoscope;
Its heart and sail wore rich motifs.

Each shop along the waterfront
Had dimmed its lamps or closed its door
All quite content new ways to shunt
And keep a wall upon that shore.
The downcast anchor of their eyes
Gave little hint this shore had need
To give the new ship's enterprise
A will to stay; or cause to plead.

And soon the ship sailed off to sea
To other ports-of-call to greet;
And left the rocks of apathy
To seek another hand to meet.
The darkened shops and empty lane
Ne'er knew the vessel turned away ...
Ne'er knew her cause nor sensed her gain ...
Ne'er saw the treasure ... lost that day.

I John 4: 7-10, 20-21

friends,
family and
other treasures

I Have Two Daughters

I have just two daughters ... two daughters ... just two,
And tall talent it seems is their name, yes their name.
They reach me, beseech me, they teach me they do,
And much do they have to acclaim, to acclaim.
And much do they have to acclaim.

I have just two daughters ... two daughters ... just two,
And I tell you that friendship's their name, yes their name.
To people and people they're friends through and through,
In sunshine or rain, they're the same, just the same.
In sunshine or rain, they're the same.

I have just two daughters ... two daughters ... just two,
And warm-hearted and kind is their name, yes their name.
They'll walk extra miles, give their shirt and their shoe,
And never a bit of it claim, would they claim.
And never a bit of it claim.

I have just two daughters ... two daughters ... just two,
And much goodness and truth is their name, yes their name.
The Lord is their guide for the life they pursue,
And lofty the point of their aim, yes their aim.
And lofty the point of their aim.

I have just two daughters ... two daughters ... just two,
And pure sweetness and true is their name, yes their name.
They're a wellspring of love and so love them I do,
Each of them more than the same, just the same.
Each of them more than the same.

A Friend

To have all gold beyond one's greatest dreams,
A fool will trust such bounty will not pass,
But when deceived truth cuts like shattered glass,
And life falls short when bent on selfish schemes.
More wise to seek a greater goal it seems,
A promise sure, *real* treasure to amass,
Exceeding every worldly gain and class,
That sees you weak and fallen yet esteems!
What more in life to have if not a friend,
To challenge us to seek the better caste,
Who'll kindly to our need and hope attend,
With daunting creed and honor holding fast.
A friend who suffers faults and ills to mend,
And stays the troubled times until the last!

John 15: 9-17

Father's Day

We know you -- you were with us long ago;
When we were small -- mere spark amid the glow,
A twinkling eye -- a touch of heaven here below.
And you -- A steady hand to help us grow.
You were called honesty and playfulness.
And we -- well we came to hug you.

When things were tough along the way,
You labored hard so we could play,
And have a home where we could stay,
And learn to love and learn to pray.
You were called integrity and perseverance.
And we -- well we came to tolerate you

Then we struggled through teen years;
Had our bumps and had our fears;
Our escapades and foamy beers;
The giddy laughs -- the ready tears.
You were called patience and hopefulness.
And we -- well we came to avoid you.

Then suddenly we're over twenty,
With lofty dreams and hopes aplenty;
And you were there to be our friend,
Through every pothole -- every bend.
You were called support and knowledge.
And we -- well we came to depend on you.

Now we have children of our own,
And in their hearts the seeds are sown,
So they too live in dreams full-blown,
With love and promise fully shown.
And you are called -- older and wiser ...
And we -- well we came to love you.

Being A Friend

In deep of night and depth of fear,
You're standing there within my room.
When sadness takes away the cheer,
Your gentle touch erases gloom.

In all those times you cured my woes,
Was subtle portent ever there,
Amid the joy where healing glows,
And happiness replaces care?

Which gift is easier to bring,
A body cured or heart restored?
What pow'r can make the spirit sing,
Made pure anew with love outpoured?

Eternity to us is brought,
Though seen by faith and love alone.
Life's pain so often called to naught,
Forgiving seeds again are sown!

In *every* person that we meet,
We're called as healed to be a friend,
The way we help, the way we greet,
Is prayer that the healed ones send!

Remain in God, remain in love,
John said the meaning is the same,
And not just in the God above,
But lonely, hungry, lost and lame!

I John 4: 7-16

"... As Thyself "

If I could serve my brother honestly,
And in that strife embrace his fear and pain,
Ne'er mindful of my loss, but of his gain,
A greater hope and spirit would I see.
I would transcend my selfish reverie,
By action breaking every bond and chain,
That holds my soul entrapped in sinful stain,
And clouds the course to true nobility.
Sad truth it is that comes before my eyes,
And robs me of my will to hear that need,
Replacing hope with resignation's sighs,
And weakened heart to sue for lesser deed.
But now my soul renewed, e'er lively tries
To once again embrace that greater creed.

Matthew 22: 34-40

The Birds Of Morning

It seems like hours ...
Sleep has spurned my company ...
Thoughts flood ...
Disparaging thoughts ...
Hope challenged ...
The night is so long ... so very long ...
Deeply dark and quiet it is ...
An overpowering presence of gloom ...
Lonely, awful loneliness ...
And then a sound ...
melodic sound ...
faintly ...
at a distance ...
Then another ...
closer ...
another ...
... closer still.
... In a moment sweet melodies are played out
... here ... over there ... and there ...
and there ...
everywhere.
Never loud, never obtrusive,
Always soothing,
Comforting.
Heralds of morning
The sun is coming. The sun is coming.
Still it is dark ... deeply dark,
But now darkness with hope ... with promise.
Amid the darkest moments
Of this darkest night,
The birds of morning have anticipated
The coming light,
Dispensing early joy from the gloom of night,
Singing their songs of happiness and joy ...
Hope rises with their humble music.
Soon the night will be over.

See the pink horizon.
See the black turn gray,
Steadily changing,
Morning light ...

Sometimes life closes in ...
It is dark ... it is long ...
It is lonely ...
and darkness spurns our dreams,
Floods us with despair,
Erodes our hope ...
Where is the music?
Where is the light?
What is that you say, Lord?
Have faith.
Hear the distant songbirds.
Hear the heralds of light.
But in this darkness it is so difficult ...
But there ... on the horizon of our lives ...
There is the Son ... our source of Light.
We know Him as brother.
Reach out to Him.
He is light.
He is hope.
He is here with us.
Let us sing our songs of happiness and joy.
The songbirds are sweetly singing ...
The dark night is soon over ...
Eye has not seen ...
Mind cannot comprehend ...
Leap for joy in faith justified ...
He is here for us ...
As He said he would be ...
Always ...

John 17:1-26

The Call to Care

If there's a nobler calling then
I haven't seen it yet.
Dressed in white with chart and pen,
A striking silhouette.

A heart of gold, a smile to match,
Her patient reigns supreme.
She moves along with swift dispatch,
The ailing to redeem.

She's selfless with a mannered poise,
While struggling through the worst,
Like music in a field of noise,
Or song superbly versed.

But though her mind is keenly trained,
The thing that shines so bright,
Is that she sees a person pained,
And joins them in their fight.

With every skill within her scope,
Her heart is ever there,
Bringing kindness ... giving hope
Through all that they must bear.

So thankfully I tip my hat,
To nurses everywhere,
Who take the time to stop and chat,
And heal us with their care.

Matthew 25: 34-46

Birdies

Behind our house where birdies fly,
My wife just loves to watch 'em.
When Squirrely eats you'll hear her sigh,
"He's here again to botch 'em!"

The blue jays say they are the boss,
The feeders empty quick.
They strut and peck and she gets cross
Each time their beak they flick.

The best part is the finches' play,
In swoopin' twos or threes,
Yellow-blue and purple-gray,
The smaller ones do please.

Even Tiny Chippie there,
Is learning to get to it.
If dogs could climb they'd come by pair,
To find that seed and chew it.

There's few things where my wife finds ire,
Except for maybe hubby.
Just crows and squirrels that feed acquire
When already they're too chubby!

Summer Day

I walked one summer day
and a tree spoke to me,
a brook sang to me,
the sun warmed my life,
an egret soared with me,
a shadowed mountain chanted quiet psalms,
and I was born anew.

Ever New

Cato lived four score and more
In classic Roman days ...
Then took up Greek ne'er learned before,
A task sure to amaze.

Socrates gave dance a fling
When most his years had passed ...
He felt his spirit lacked the ring
Of movement that would last.

Roget lived on to ninety-two
Comparing word to word ...
A daunting task for him to do
Though really not absurd.

John Glenn went soaring past his prime
To view from outer space
A world of changes in his time
That make a better place.

As life gets long and days get short,
We need to look within ...
And find a newness we can court,
To make us young again ...

A Christmas Prayer

We think of the things of Christmas past,
The carols, the snow ... some toy.
We think of the things that really last,
The children, the love and the joy.

We think of the reason we celebrate,
This season that lifts hearts so.
We think of Jesus and concentrate,
On His love and the challenge to grow.

The greatest night of the year ... tonight,
We each feel in our innermost way,
Moved to our depths by that Spiritual Light,
We reflect and we pause here to pray.

We thank you, O Lord, as we share this meal,
For your gifts beyond our reciting,
Family and friends and things we can feel,
For times quiet ... and times also exciting.

So humbly we pause for a moment or two,
As in silence we quietly pray,
Our own heartfelt praise and thanksgiving to you,
For giving us this Christmas Day.

Luke 2: 1-14

faith —
the lights
in the
darkness

Cosmos And Chaos

There it was ... faithless and in time begot ...
A gift ... an essence from an unknown god ...
Fleshy unmolded life ... a scrap of sod,
With unremembered past ... moving ... to what?
Splintered species ... conflicted, misty plot ...
Drawn by nature as peas in broken pod ...
A path walked both with curse and virtue shod ...
Guided by an inner calling ... to what?
Enough order ... this chaos to survive?
Enough wisdom ... this cosmos to conceive?
Enough thought ... to ask why we're here alive?
Enough hope ... to venture? ... to believe?
Enough doubt ... each byte to question and to skive?
Enough love ... to find forever in life's weave?

True Purpose

To what true purpose is man's life ordained,
And how such brief duration thus explained?
What is the reach and vision that is life?
Is sole cause merely fleeting joy and strife,
One instant born and thence borne on to die,
The only end a sad and tearful eye?

Would God in lofty irony waste power,
And short measure to us mete as our Endower?
Would He not in man seek some reflection,
Of free will giv'n back to Vast Perfection?
Have we no measure justly to compare ...
Some gift of ours reflecting back *our* care?

God a purpose and a wisdom does impart,
That we should know the depth within His heart.
That with His awesome pow'r a side so mild
That He would *share* creation in *each* child,
And we would come to know the goodness of
The gift of giving life that's borne of love.

Within our children we are wont to see
Love will not stop short of eternity...
How even more our God Omniscient
Would see our hopes as heart-felt testament,
Reflecting back some breadth and depth of love,
And faith within that knows the source thereof.

Love that is with patience and in kindness found,
Love that to the humble way and truth is bound,
That neither jealousy nor rudeness rails,
That bears and hopes all things and never fails.
To what true purpose is man's life ordained?
'Tis love ...
in endless measure ...
ne'er contained ...

Body, Mind And Soul

I sat amid the trees and birds and myriad wild,
Musing how body, mind and soul be reconciled.
It seemed all within that woods had finite quality,
Each nature clearly known within its family tree.
Does a bird fancy more than nature freely gives?
Or tree to seek a change from where it ever lives?
In each of living nature's beings we know and see,
There are limits, ways and beauties ... that make them free.
Of those multitude of actions we know them by,
We ne'er could change one whit no matter how we try.
Each being has a plan to which it is resigned.
But man ... with godly gifts is yet to be defined.

He struggles with the blend of body, mind and soul,
A balance there he seeks to optimize the whole.
Mind slower than the flesh progresses with some pain,
E'er grasping outlived thoughts and knowledge kept in vain.
And yet there's innate restlessness that man pursues,
Ne'er quenched with present state but untread path would choose!
And greatest of the three and master of one's fate,
The soul commands them all and calls them to be great.
It seeks that vein that brings the spirit rich appeal,
Then dares it often as it would with avid zeal.
Allows no fetters by idea, place or man,
But quests for truth and love and virtue as it can.

One needs a constant bedrock home from which to soar ...
The Paraclete ... that ever draws to distant shore,
To place where there's neither race nor sex nor rage,
But truth that lifts, accepts and binds o'er age on age.
The Spirit holds in trust for each and all to share,
That blend of body, mind and soul held in His care!
What boundaries then be set for man, what limits brought,
What harmony of mind and soul and body sought?
The Spirit guides each man from deepest depths within,
And asks that man live much in love and not in sin ...
Such guidance deigns that body, mind and soul will be
In perfect blend before Love's awesome majesty!

Calling Forth

Its pull ever-present ... no pause ... no rest ...
Irresistible ... hour by hour ...
As close as the breath in our labored chest,
Or the fragrance of June in the flower.
Mortality fading ... time's dying light ...
There ... right before us ... straight on ... with no brakes;
Constantly moving - through pleasure and blight,
Passive as leaves to its turbulent wakes ...
Each present moment thrust into the past,
Burning our dreams into embers gone cold;
Jewels of a lifetime too quickly surpassed,
It lies there unchanged ... while soon we are old.
There in our path it stays, never resting,
Taking the time and spending and spending.
Beckoning forth our hopes and our questing,
A vortex ... a flood ... ever impending.
Passing all things ... to remain e'er the same ...
Of'fring us only mystery and cloud;
Ne'er quenched, it draws forth from certainty's claim ...
Compelling us toward its darkly veiled shroud.
Through many veils ... ethereal calling,
Our fear and its brothers have no account,
As flotsome bows to flood waters falling,
In whispered murmur or loud roaring shout ...
Relentless holder of time ... on it goes ...
More certain than death ... unyielding as shale ...
We ... like the leaves the white water swallows,
Pass through its mists quickly ... veil after veil.

Each passing alters the beauty a shade ...
Slowly ... unnoticed ... as inward we're turned.
The youthful ... the sparkling soft colors fade,
Like wrinkled, worn parchment ... tattered and burned ...
And beauty finds new life deep in the heart,
To grow and to flourish ... within heaven's love;
And aging reveals a mind ... saged and apart;
Tried and grown strengthened from Wisdom above.

Passing all passing ... and ages and time ...
Beyond all the eons ... where faith becomes sure,
Where Virtue is awesome and Wonder sublime ...
Where hope with its head raised, holds Wisdom secure ...
Eternity's threshold ... victory won ...
The last veil now lifted ... timeless the scope.
And lo ... Love is found ... so great as to stun ...
Love ... greater than faith ... surpassing all hope!

I Corinthians 13: 8-13

Regret

Too often do we dwell within that space,
Where pride and ego claim our inner core;
Where greed would have us seek for even more,
While time for others' needs be but a trace.
Too often would we noble act displace,
To seek those things we rightly should abhor,
Amid still beauty lost in trifle's roar,
While we a lesser consciousness embrace.
Could we disaster find by such poor claim,
When we by stages still the Spirit's call;
When we in sloth bring godliness to shame,
While blithely setting sure our fateful fall?
When all is done, what tragic fate we'll claim;
That we turned silent conscience to it all!

Morning Mass

In Erin's shore at County Clare
On misty stone walled lane,
From fog, the early morn breaks fair,
To light the brae and plain.

A camping group of youths depart
In Arizona heat,
To seek and learn the desert chart,
And help some folks they meet.

Along the gray de Fuca Straight,
All veiled within the cloud,
The lonely steeple bells create,
A calling through the shroud.

Across the straight -- across the sea,
In every town and class,
They walk the mists in amity,
Going to morning Mass.

Friendly faces, shining hope,
Bring light to early day,
Humble faith of global scope,
That welcomes emigre.

Eucharist

Many said, "This saying is hard".
Many won't believe it.
The bread ... the wine ... real flesh ... real blood ...
In faith do we receive it.

He said He'll raise those of that faith
Upon the last of days;
"I am the bread of life", He said,
With faith comes change of ways.

Such love we cannot comprehend;
The humble we ignore.
That God, rebuffed ... would suffer all;
Man's future to restore.

"Whoever eats my flesh", He said,
"And drinks my blood remains ..."
"In me and I in him." His words,
The words that man disdains.

In mystery He comes to us
To Live there deep inside;
And change our outlook to new heights
Where peace and love reside.

The proud ... the mighty ... may reject
The eucharistic call,
But John is clear -- with this neglect,
You'll have no life at all ! *

*John 6: 22-69

Martyrs

To most it seems a terrible twist,
A child so young and fair would die,
That taken ere the prime of life
Would soon in quiet meadow lie.
To most it is a test of faith;
How could a good God so ordain?
But in this world where nothing lasts,
It takes The Timeless to explain.

As next to awesome ocean's breadth
The bountied brook small measure is;
Our life on earth its joys and gain,
No match to heaven's treasure is.
Those martyred souls before us died,
And showed by courage this was true.
Their lives of faith when sorely tried,
No demon could with fear undo.

How can we judge what God will give
To any victim on death's door?
He told us, "Trust and you will live!"
And most did trust who've gone before.
We've seen them die with serene bliss,
As though they saw a vision there,
Within their eyes a parting kiss,
Their fading breath a final prayer.

Questions

Have you a temple made to God?
Is it made of gold or sod?
Can you touch its deity?
Has it close proximity?
Is your temple in the sky?
Does it hear you when you cry?
Has it some reality?
Does it help your soul to see?

Is your temple in the leaves;
In the scenes that nature weaves?
Is your temple in the streams?
Is it present in your dreams?
Is its texture flesh and blood?
Heart and feelings? Brotherhood?
Does it bleed of blood or oil?
Will it last or will it spoil?

Does it help you when you're blue?
Does it help you struggle through
All that life holds ... every share?
All that leads one to despair?
When your final act is done
Will it rise like setting sun?
Then within it, will you see
Pain and anguish gone from thee?

Has your temple truth and hope?
Has it love of endless scope?
Think awhile ... reveal to me ...
What your temple means to thee.
What is in your temple's walls?
Is it mystic truth that calls?
Tell me what your temple's like ...
I'm a pilgrim on this pike ...

"Be still!" ... the silent voice revealed
Secrets that my pride had sealed ...
A clarity ... a power flowed,
An inner light of wisdom glowed ...
"In everything the Father gives
Are temples where His presence lives;
But greatest temple you will find
Is in your body, soul and mind!"

Dot Com

This unique altered string ... cut and pasted,
To reside in future time ... future space;
A million point four bytes all in a row;
A trillion times these millions ... *then it's gone!*
In a flick ... erased ... gone beyond UNDO;
Just vanished ... the new address has no DOT COM.
"This is a non-recoverable error."
"That altered string is now write protected" ...
"There will be no more changes in this text" ...
"Press any key to continue" ... Now what?
"It is now safe to turn off this device" ...
Can any creature find this altered text?
The power is off ... electrons are still ...
"This is a non-recoverable error."
Did the hard drive crash? Can Maker be called?
Where has it gone ... this unique altered string?
Somewhere in the universe there is an answer.
Amen

Holy Night

In the cold of a clear night -- with stars everywhere,
Like nights we have all seen and felt and shivered in;
There is a sense of a special Presence in the sky
That the humble ones will come to see --
The shepherds, the lowly animals, a quiet man,
And a poor, heavily-laden teenage girl ... his wife.
Their breath visible in the dim light of their shelter,
They settle in for the harsh and painful reality of childbirth.
No doctors ... no anesthesia ... nothing and no one to ease the pain ...
No armies ... no fanfares ... no lofty personages there to help ...
Just the quiet ... and the cold ... and the Presence ...
The pain ... the moans ... are heard only by this quiet man.
And then ... by the humility of this teenager ...
highly blessed by the Almighty;
In that most humble of surroundings;
In a dung-filled place we would not rest
Even for an hour, let alone a night ...
The Son of Man chooses to breathe his first breath
Of the air of earth ... in the company of the poor ...
Wrapped in the most meager of wrappings;
The God of Power and Might,
The God of unspeakable Love,
Comes among us as a helpless babe ...
... Emanuel ...
... God is with us ...
To bring us eternal peace.
And all the cold and clear and starry nights thereafter
Will silently echo the angels' chorus
Of that first Christmas;
And that Presence that was beheld in the sky that night,
Will speak quietly but powerfully,
Within our hearts,
Forever.

The Rear View Mirror

You know God is in your rear view mirror,
If e'er you doubt His nearness.
You need not be some mystic seer,
To focus Him in clearness.

Just look at life and where you've come,
If you're to see His caring ...
Children and a loving home,
And all those friends for sharing.

No, you don't need brilliance of the mind
To know He's been there near you.
Where you were will help you find,
His presence there in clear view.

John 6: 37-40

A Prayer At Five A.M.

Would you sleep, when storm and thunder burn inside?
Slumber thee my soul, when others' hope is sorely tried?
Go forth, 'tis time to love ...
See ... Your brother calls to thee.
That challenge deep within is from above ...
You must respond and hear his plea ...
The time is short ... his anguish awesome deep.
Later there'll be time enough to sleep.
Be still ... reflect ... hear his faint and distant call ...
Before it fades.

Nothing

Would you say I'm nothing, God?
I've never saved a life ...
Would you say I'm nothing, God?
I've little healed the strife.
Would you say I'm nothing, God?
I've often added pain ...
Would you say I'm nothing, God?
I've little eased the strain.

You *would* say I'm something, Lord.
So long as I keep trying ...
You *would* say I'm something, Lord.
So much ... You suffered dying!
May I to others' nothingness,
Be hopeful friend and kind ...
May I to others' nothingness,
Their shining beauty find!

Pilgrim

The first man has spoken to God ...
And the first man is connected to the last ...
Because the first awakens in turn the last,
Who will again speak to God ...

And Wisdom whispers ...
Come ... seek what is to be.

He soars the sky ... leaves footprints in the dusty mare;
Marveling at what is done;
Looks back to a blue marble set in pitch;
Sees new mysteries begun.

Stands watch as the potion works its cure;
Marveling at what is done;
Looks into the eyes that had been death;
Sees new mysteries begun.

And Wisdom whispers ...
Come ... seek what is to be.

He inspires with every sweep of brush,
Every turn of word,
Every thrill of song ...
Still ... endless ... more bounty waits ...

He travels all labyrinths ...
Yet nowhere in that great sweep
Does he ... a spirit grasp,
Or a soul pluck from its very origins ...

Or even reveal where that was,
Or whither it came from,
Or how it was held together there with life
... that great unknown ...

And Wisdom whispers ...
Come ... seek what is to be.

He dwells at the foot of the mountain,
But is shown the heights;
Is but a small creature in a vast ocean,
But is taught the mastery of the depths;
Walks in ignorance in a forest of grandeur,
But is given inner peace to savor it;
Alone in the dark of night,
But has a hand to reach and touch;
Tires before reaching all he needs or wishes,
But is given place and time to rest,
And mind to learn,
And spirit to know why,
And to yearn
To be one ...

And Wisdom whispers ...
Come ... seek what is to be.

And all of this was while he slept ...
... Before he awakened ...

Psalm 8: 4-10

Dreams and Clouds

There's a whole wide world in those clouds up there,
I see faces with smiles and dreams so fair,
The breeze blows them fast in that fresh, clean air,
In my dreams rest I in my upward stare ...

You make no lament of the strife below,
Whether rich man or poor, you do not know,
Just a race to the distance ... Blow, wind blow!
Goodly place to a far-off land you go.

May I join in your fancy in the sky?
May I go where your dreams go by and by?
Would you lift my dreams when the end is nigh ...
To a happy place where no more will die?

Conversation

I saw you walking by the sea.
Was I alone? Were you with me?
I saw you there with heavy heart.
Had you and I then grown apart?

I saw you standing by the stream.
What was I doing in that dream?
I washed your soul; I washed it clean.
Were you present, but unseen?

I saw you praying in the night.
Was I afraid of heaven's light?
You seemed so pensive in the dark.
Did then my soul reveal its mark?

I do believe remorse I read.
Was that the reason joy had fled?
You were forgiven, don't you know.
There's so much crimson in the snow!

I'm with you walking by the sea.
Is that your guiding hand on me?
I hear you clearly when you speak.
Even when I'm soiled and weak?

When you are pensive, cold and down ...
See you a man, or just a clown?
I see in you a piece of me ...
Will you remain eternally?

Isaiah 58: 1-9

The Good Thief

"This day you shall be with me in Paradise."

Can it be true? Is this really happening?
Yes, it *is* true -- it *is* happening -- it *is* real! He's saying these words
to *you* !
-- Overwhelming awe.
What fantastic words to hear and to know in your heart they are true.
But the agony!

Crucifixion!

Fighting the weight of the body against the nails penetrating the
hands and feet.
Excruciating pain. Unimaginable pain.
Continually growing weakness and thirst and fever,
then chills and buzzing in the ears, failing vision, extreme nausea,
stark loneliness, the sureness of death immediately at hand,
frontal confrontation by all of the powers of darkness,
a sense of total helplessness,
an overpowering desire for death to end this terrible suffering,
The certainty that these are the last moments of life on earth.
Fear, doubt, shame, regret.
No comforting touch.
No soothing drug.
No power of the will.
No returning to the familiar things of this world.
No more second chances.
Done ... Finished ... Over ...
Prayers that were coursing through the lips
like the water of a cloudburst rushing through a culvert are now
slowing.
At first, the lips moved as if to whisper the prayers,
but soon there is no longer strength left to even move the lips

and the prayers are only mental images -- fading mental images.
Then the fading of pain -- lessening of dizziness. And the hope ...
... as the words play again and again through the core of one's being

"This day you shall be with me in Paradise."

Helplessness falls away as the warmth of love rushes to console and comfort.
A life force beyond anything ever experienced becomes palpable
even as the length of each dying breath gets longer and longer
until there is no breath left at all.
And breath is replaced by peace and light and the power that is so pure.
And, at once, one feels the love filling and purifying every dark vestige left within.

Quiet -- Quiet -- Quiet and peacefulness.
Total tranquility devoid of any hint of anything negative.
Time hanging as if it no longer existed.
Just one single huge moment of stillness and serenity ...

Forgiven ...

Thy will be done ...

Forever ...

Luke 23: 35 - 43

Neither Here Nor There

I saw a man with bandaged heart
And homeless was his name ...
He asked me nothing ... went his way,
And I remained the same.

He did not ask ... I did not act
And homeless he remained ...
His flesh was mask ... I'll never know
How deeply he was pained.

There was a storm that took his home,
His family and his wife ...
I wished him well and kept on goin'
And let him live his life.

I spoke of all the good I'd done
But never knew *his* care ...
Because he never asked my help
'Twas neither here nor there.

I hope the Lord will always wait
For me to ask *His* name ...
And say it's neither here nor there
I passed Him ... lost and lame ...

Matthew 25: 31-46

Sinner

Out of my sin call me, Lord,
For weak I would despair,
For proud I would declare,
"Was not *my* fault for strident chord,
Was not *my* act to be abhorred".

From my sloth show me higher road,
For weak I would not rise,
For proud, seek paths unwise,
In darkness find abode,
And in vague hues the goodness won ... erode.

Set my path aright to Thy ways,
For strong I'll rise anew,
In light, dark deeds undo,
Once more repentant heart ablaze
In acts and words that sing your praise.

Out of my sin lift me, O God,
In you alone I'm saved,
No more to sin enslaved.
Forgiveness be my staff and rod,
Wisdom's light ... the guiding path I trod.

John 8: 3-11

Discerning

I don't know how I should discern
God's will for me to find and learn,
Perhaps it's due to my strong will,
Or maybe that my mind's not still.
Whatever reason that it is,
I fear I choose my will ... not His!

One Way Only

Mem'ry alone visits the days gone by,
Our recall alone travels back.
Set firmly in stone does every day die,
Time travels a single way track.

If it's your wish to set yesterday right,
There's just one way you can do it ...
Do rightly today before it's tonight,
That's all there really is to it.

You can't remake what you did yesterday,
So don't even give it a thought,
Just do better today and virtue display,
Rememb'ring the lesson it taught!

the
lighter side

✦ ✦ ✦ ✦ ✦ ✦ ✦

Be A Kind Critic

If you are a friend of mine,
And look upon my work,
Be honest as you read each line,
True judgment never shirk.

But if you think its *really* bad,
And don't know what to say,
More gas to fire do not add,
Let silence be your way.

My skin, you see, is fairly thick,
And I can stand the truth,
'Specially if your rhetoric,
Is mixed with sweet vermouth.

So read it over ... take a look ...
And have some fun with it ...
But put some sugar on the hook
Before you're done with it.

My Friend -- The Bogeyman

My friend he is a patient man
Except when on the links.
He'll spend two days to fix a fan
And very rarely drinks.

The game of golf will patience test,
That surely is the case,
And folks with meager talent blessed,
Embarrassment will face.

And when good fortune looks away
Their drives go left and right,
To trap and pond and sloping brae,
It's not a pretty sight.

It starts unraveling the nerves,
And butchers calm composure,
When drives are all assorted curves,
And par escapes exposure.

Correct address to little sphere
The club don't always follow,
So birds and beasties quake in fear,
And flee to closest hollow.

His drive traverses north to east
And rockets toward the thicket
A blur to every man and beast
A bullet couldn't lick it!

"Lord!" he says." FORE!" HE SHOUTS,
His shot flung from that muzzle.
The problem is its whereabouts,
What gopher's hole to nuzzle.

Then softly putted little ball,
A-creepin' 'cross the grass,
Propelled so slow it takes three shots,
That four-inch cup to pass!

And when it gets to yonder hole
And rims around the lip,
The neck veins throb like glowing coal,
You're sure he's gonna flip.

Sad it is that little ball
Can rule that sturdy guy,
And make him vow to one and all
He'd counted every lie.

When each and all they knew for sure
He *never* shot that low.
Just like the man with pole and lure
'Twas stretched scenario.

But do we care a nit or two
When friendship is at stake,
Were he to take a false kudo
And lower numbers make?

Imagine playin' in a game
Where *zero's* the ideal score,
Where no one's even filed a claim
To *forty-six* before.

I say we should forbearance wear
To those who ply the links,
Just playin's quite a hefty share
O sufferin', me thinks.

Arthur And His Friends

You say you've now got ar - thur - ri - tis aplenty,
And vision 'long time ago left twenty-twenty,
Ya can't eat them bonbons or other real good things,
And when you git up ya sound like a frog sings.
O yes me ole friend-ee you're just gettin' older,
When that ache in your back has annexed your left shoulder.

If the vim you're a gettin' comes from a pink pill,
And before it's eight-thirty your energy's nil,
What you do is you dedicate all of those places,
That have youthful zip though it be just in traces,
You maximize even the slightest of pluses,
Ne'er letting on any of what all the fuss is.

You can't put the brakes on Ole Father Time's march
When your bod gits to rustin' plumb out of its starch,
You just have to sit there and grin and you bear it,
Maybe find you a pal with whom you can share it.
Because don't you know it won't get any better,
So grit them false teeth firm and don't be a fretter.

Now maybe you'll say it's all very concernin',
Your uneasy sleep fraught with tossin' and turnin'.
When recallin' this mornin's a hit and miss shootin',
And butterin' toast well nigh hard executin'.
It's rough, tough and fatnin' and darn frus-ter-ray-tin,
And if that ain't enough it's hu - mil - e - a - tin'.

So what can we do, elder sisters and brothers?
Geriatric maladies sure ain't our druthers.
I say, look straight ahead at this ugly invader,
And say, "Look here, you party poopin' crusader,
I've got lotsa stuff left ... my wit and my humor,
And innermost strength, you insidious roomer."

So maybe I'll hurt and not hear all that good,
And maybe not do all the things that I would,
But I'll tell you right now I'm not givin' in,
I'm pushin' and pushin' and pushin' agin'.
With the Lord at my side and hope to impart,
I'll keep right on keepin' a smile in my heart.

Now What?

"I'm sorry to say
That there's bad news today,
We're unsure of your future condition.
Your carotid's a mess,
Dark days coming unless,
We reverse this sad supposition."

As the doctor reviewed,
Those symptoms all skewed,
Like the track of a sinister particle ...
My mind wandered away,
To an earlier day,
When my bod was a number one article.

That night sleep came in fits,
Good thoughts ground into bits,
Even I surmised heavy insomnia.
When I drifted to sleep,
A darkly veiled creep,
Asked, "You want that I now should embalm ya?"

I said, "Thanks just the same,
I'm not ready to claim,
My place in the heavenly dwelling ...
Because as you speak,
Though my body is weak,
Your persuasion's not all that compelling."

"So please take your leave
'cuz I truly believe,
Your authority's very suspicious ...
I have things I must do,
And they don't involve you,
Plus your timing seems very capricious."

"So, come morning I'll go,
To the specialist's show,
Not expecting to find panaceas ...
Just a reasonable chance,
Rosy cheeks to enhance
By seeking his latest ideas."

Back To The Sod

I'd like to go to Erin's land,
To where there's sweet and honey.
I been there once before y'know,
'Twas 'fore I left me money ...

I left me work a bit too soon,
Or so it would appear;
I'd probably now be sittin' there,
Had I worked another year.

But then life's fickle, as you know,
We're all a bit too swift,
To change our venue and our life,
And set ourselves adrift.

But me Mother's past is in me blood;
It beckons me to come
To where the leprechauns abound,
And enchantment comes to some.

And so to caution I will say,
"Good mornin' to ye, sir!
I tink me leave I'll be a-takin'
Whilst me body still can stir."

So off I'm goin' real soon, ya know,
To Ireland's green hills.
I'll worry when I do return
To face those unpaid bills.

Yuk ... Phone Sales!

Wynkin', Blynkin' and Nod ... my ole friends,
Were happily kicking about some loose ends,
When rudely they're jousted from out of the deep,
Of a sweetly enjoyable heavenly sleep.

A bell ringing faintly grew steadily louder,
Breaking the fog like dynamite powder.
Rising quickly, I'm hearing the water glass fall,
With its contents now covering half of the wall.

I mumbled some words spoken just when alone,
While grappling so crudely to pick up the phone.
"Hello there" wasn't the thing on my mind,
But I tried to be pleasant if not all that kind.

A syrupy voice spoke quickly a pitch;
Only my name was muffed even a glitch.
My moniker murdered beyond all correcting,
The spiel sped along all mortals neglecting.

When after a spate of most patient replies,
It was clear that the voice would not take my "good- byes"
I did what my upbringing said was quite rude,
In mid-sentence cut off their means to intrude.

So here's a fair warning, ye telephone hawkers,
The next time you call ... won't be any talkers.
I'm fixin' a bell with a siren and honkers,
To answer your spiel ... and make *YOU* go bonkers!

Just A Regular Guy

I eat my meals at prescribed times,
I use the bathroom every day,
I never smoke or miss my rhymes,
And just on certain days I play.
All stuff needs routine don't you know,
And boring does your lifetime go.

Breakfast time is juice and oats,
And seldom is there cake or pie,
Avoiding all the stuff that bloats,
So friends and folks won't say, "Oh my!"
All stuff needs routine don't you know,
And boring does your lifetime go.

Each day I walk a mile or two,
I do it whether heat or rain,
I do it in the snow and flu,
Persistence 'spite of ache or pain.
All stuff needs routine don't you know,
And boring does your lifetime go.

The side bar of this daily drone,
I'm just a terribly boring guy,
Makin' sure I don't condone,
The spare tire going to twenty ply.
All stuff needs routine don't you know,
And boring does your lifetime go.

If things go well and I should find,
The first hotel past pearly gate,
I have some questions on my mind,
Like how they schedules regulate.
And does stuff need a routine there?
If yes ... then check me in elsewhere.

Lifetime Guarantee!

Once upon a time (as time is often told),
I bought a timepiece at a bargain store;
A lifetime guarantee was claim so bold,
'T'would challenge even skinflint to the core!

Now most of us have need to know the hour,
To order life and fill each day with glee;
But lifetime products tend to make me sour,
To know they have more ticks in them than me!

News Of The Day

I used to watch the Evening News,
And once bought morning papers;
But then repeated tales were clues
That sad and tragic capers
Are oft-repeated tales of woe,
With little gleeful passion;
And I would really rather know
What stocks to put my stash in!

Rain

The drops move gently down the pane,
The sill would seem their final gain,
Some drops racing,
Some slow pacing,
More and more join their refrain.

You hear their footsteps on the roof,
A million hucksters on the hoof,
Some tread lightly,
Some more might'ly,
So good this barn is waterproof.

A voice came to me in the haze,
"What a good day just to laze.
Skies so weepy,
Aren't you sleepy?"
I sez, "Love these rainy days!"

"You will not have to mow today
And put those rakes and hoes away"
Plans now altered,
Action haltered,
Time called due to heav'nly spray.

This *does* seem good time for a nap,
But oops! Was that a thunderclap?
It sounds quite near,
Too close I fear,
Was that a branch I just heard snap?

With all those trees above my head,
Should I to better shelter tread?
"You will get wet,
That's one sure bet."
Another clap, I quickly fled.

So close I felt my hobnails fuse,
So much for taking me a snooze,
Now in full flight,
Like laser light,
I'm heading for a nip o' booze.

Quickly poured myself a jigger,
Second branch fell -- even bigger,
Heard the smash,
An ugly crash,
Sounded like a cannon trigger!

Right where the little barn had stood,
Was tools and spools and piles o' wood,
Were I still there,
My spouse so fair
Would now be tastin' widowhood!

My Job List grew another chore,
A task that wasn't there before,
It must be done,
Won't be no fun,
New shed for junk and stuff galore.

The drops can't find the broken pane,
No sill there now -- just acid rain,
Some drops racing,
Some slow pacing,
More and more join their refrain.

And now that crystal beauty's o'er,
The nap time gone with broken mower,
A splintered shed,
And me 'most dead,
And nine lives clearly down to FOUR!

A Gone Fishin' Birthday

When e'er there's time to rest a while
And take the lure and pole,
You'll find him sneakin' off in style
To test that fishin' hole.

It may not feed the girls and him
A single meal it's true,
'Cuz all those scrawny bass and brim
Would scarce fill barbecue.

Who cares a brown fig anyway
If any fish are bitin'.
The fun is in the sunny day
And are the buggers' fightin'.

If on this day the candle glow
Gets brighter than the sun,
Ya might just have to take and go
And leave the party fun.

If all the years stack up to be
A downer to your outlook,
Ya might just have to go and see
If you can make a trout hook!

We'll all be still awaitin' here
To see ya comin' back,
With smiles a grinnin' ear to ear,
The big one in the sack.

Now that's a birthday sure to please
And toot the sousaphone,
To know you got the biggest cheeze
The pond had ever grown!

Days

Life is metered short in days
Though we make little of it.
Quite finite time to change our ways
And see what lies above it.

Five thousand days brings teenage years
That lead us to the rest;
The joys, the growth and all the fears
That show us what is best.

If marriage is one's path to choose,
Eight thousand days we count.
They pass so quickly we refuse
To see the short amount.

The golden years end well below
The thirty thousandth noon;
And soon thereafter, don't you know
You'll hear the harpist's tune.

So when you hear, "a day or two
Won't hurt you much ... if any."
Remember, life's a gift to you
Of days ... and not that many!

Aches

Tonight I feel like ninety-two
Though I'm but sixty-four;
It's like I'm comin' down with flu
And everythin' is sore.

I feel some oddness in my flesh
That scares me just a bit,
My fresh eggs really ain't so fresh
But spoiled, I won't admit.

With wheezin' nose, the air I suck
Is murder gettin' in ...
It sounds as though a rubber duck
Ate nitroglycerine.

With wobbly thuds, I weakly trot
To johnnie in the night ...
I'm sure my plumbin's gone to pot
'Cuz nothin's water-tight.

In bed I toss and sit up straight,
My body won't relax
Sufficient to negotiate
The ninety winks it lacks.

By mornin', stooped, I meet the dawn
Like primates never should,
And bend and creek and cough and yawn,
And curse my human-hood.

And when I think the worst is past,
And things are lookin' up,
My upper plate by sneeze is cast
To waiting coffee cup.

Some say it's childish antics when
They see the things I do;
I grit my teeth and count to ten;
When facts they misconstrue.

To them I say, "Around the bend,
You don't know what *you'll* reap;
So while you can, I recommend
Your comments please to keep!"

hope and
healing

If Only

If only words like candle glow
Could set your soul afire,
And give you lofty dreams to know,
And pain and fear retire.
If only I could write of things
That live within my being,
With words true inspiration brings
And lifts your heart to seeing ...

The hope I have, the joy and dreams,
I'd happily impart
The inner peace, the faith, it seems,
Was with me from the start.
If only I could write of things,
The wonders that I've seen,
Of moments given eagle's wings,
And vistas rich and clean ...

I'd write of mountains, stars and sea;
The moon's enchanting light,
When snow has softly blessed the tree,
And hushed the quiet night.
I'd write of blessings just to know
A sick child now is well;
And how his mother, eyes aglow,
Would worried thoughts dispel.

But mostly what I'd write about
Is how it's come to be;
That woven neatly all throughout,
A hand was leading me.
I can't explain it plain you see,
Though vestiges are clear;
Their trace seen retrospectively,
Emerging year by year.

Hope

Life when fully sculpted
Is as a road long built,
Stretching forth to larger vision ...
Finite, patched and tattered as a quilt.

Once lived, no force on earth
Its crooked course can set astraight;
No person, wish, or prayer
Alter long encumbered state.

And yet ... though blurred and unkept
Be its final craft less stroke and flight,
Hope and faith keep heaven open at death's gate;
A blemished image set by God aright.

Matthew 24: 13

The Miracle Of Healing

In quiet times, thoughts come to tell
Of dark times we have managed well;
Of how we struggled to succeed,
Of how our wounds all ceased to bleed.
A prayer blessed us then, my friend,
A prayer brought those times to end.

'Twas gift just in the doctors' hands,
The curing solely their commands?
When deep within they know it's true
'Tis limited what they can do.
But you and I ... we know ... my friend
Just Who it was that helped us mend.

When we were fearful of our plight,
Stark shadow in the darkened night;
Who was it with us in the gloom?
Who was it there in lonely room?
Yes ... you and I ... we know, my friend,
We know the healing prayers send.

And then those trials were put to flight,
With faith and hope that burned so bright.
We saw the healing work transcend,
But tried in vain to comprehend;
Though deep inside ... we *knew* ... my friend,
Just Who it was that helped us mend.

So now you've entered one more time,
A darkened, fearful paradigm ...
Your faith in Healing's grace once more,
Your lively spirit will restore.
There is no doubting now, my friend,
With Jesus near ... this too will end!

John 14: 12-14

-133-

Columbine Reflection

Between the ordered enclaves where we live,
An ego, torn, is moved to realms of mind
That rage at real or visioned foes ... and give
A darkened field of images that bind
His soul to ways unwilling to forgive ...
Where is the listening of ear and heart?
Where is the moderating voice to mend?
An action damned, but how, Lord, did it start?
No other way this awful plot could end?
How did a kindred soul grow so apart?

The young, now broken, lie where peace should be,
And prayers flood ... where prayers are not allowed ...
The guns of rage have killed tranquility,
And once again wrought tears ... A dreadful shroud
Stills youthful hopes and dreams of things-to-be.
And we begin anew the search to find
Some clue, some cause, some reason to believe
With all technology ... collective mind
With knowledge gained will claim a sure reprieve
That bloodied days and hate now lie behind ...

Truth is ... that apathy ... and guns ... and hate,
Without the humble prayer ... the open heart ...
Without a wisdom borne of love to advocate
For change to kinder ways that hope impart,
Will soon again those ordered enclaves desecrate.
So here we humbly kneel ... before the cross of
Broken hopes, and unlived dreams ... At the tomb
Where life is born anew! Oh God above
We ask Your strength to meet this passioned call;
This foe to greet with love, with love, with love!

Facing Depression

My thoughts were black, my spirit weak
The humor gone, the outlook bleak.
I found not much of self or joy --
Through wearied eyes I'd lost the boy
That once was there. What filled my life
Was sleepless nights and days of strife.

I tried and failed myself to right,
Repeatedly falling into night.
Night of endless self-remorse,
Night of fruitless, aimless course,
Night of hopeless distance from
Any hand to help me some.

But then a glimmer shone anew.
I sensed that others loved and knew
That I was worth the extra mile,
That I to them could bring a smile.
A measured increment each day
Of restoration came to stay.

Slow -- and sometimes slower still,
Came strengthening of mind and will.
A question to my mind arose,
"Others need you -- don't you know?
You must believe your dignity,
Has value for eternity.

You have a gift that's yours alone,
You're not just someone else's clone,
And if you leave this wretched sphere,
You'll break a heart -- evoke a tear ...
But more than that ... you'll leave a space,
Unique amid this troubled place."

The Long Night

How long it is the quiet of this night,
Alone, awake and prey to each faint sound,
A wish, a hope slight glint soon more would found,
And fading stardust greet the morning light.
O dark and silent foe to ear and sight,
You'd steal from troubled soul and peace confound,
With sleepless silence bid your spell surround,
Bring time halting and slow its darkened flight.
Dark times of life which hold each moment long
And cast a pall o'er tidings of new morn,
Wouldst take the lilting music from life's song,
And play a dirge to distant hope forlorn.
Take heart! The Lord sends forth kind hand so strong ...
'Midst darkest night is heaven's light soon born!

Meditation For A Sleepless Night

If sleep is not to come tonight, then speak to me, O Lord,
Let my long and lonesome hours be in your close accord,
Cast within my deepest soul a light for me to see
In clearest ring of truth and love just what you want of me.

The Bouquet

They came together richly
In that tinted vase of blue,
A harmony that blended
A bright and cheerful tone,
They spoke a gentle hymn there
Of fresh scent and subtle hue,
And gave back smiling sunlight
With each sparkle it had shone.
We wish you well ... your darkness ceased.
Your hope restored ... your joys released.
We are your thanks, your blessing psalm;
A healing and consoling balm.

Our Pain --Their Pain

Each day, five thousand steps of pain,
Keep me from even worse.
So suck it up, and don't complain,
It's not that bad a curse.
Other millions more do suffer,
Greater woes by far;
No one there, no caring buffer ...
No faith ... no healing scar.

No easy thousand steps and more,
Their lot to struggle through;
Just inching blood and fear and war,
And souls on barbecue.
Their children fall, their hope soon gone,
Like Job's, a dire lot.
No rest, no cure, no saving dawn,
No scraps from Camelot.

Each day, the nails burn in their cross,
Their hopes hung there to die;
Past hunger ... past all hurt and loss,
No will left, asking, "Why?"
Humility no weakness is,
When pain brings man to heel;
That once so sure uniqueness his,
Now gone like melted steel.

"My God, you have forsaken me!"
Must surely be his cry;
"I'm dripping blood here on this tree,
And wishing I would die.
Will comfort come? Will peace arrive?
Will you, Lord, heal the wound?
Will I again find love alive,
My soul again attuned?"

But here we are. Our comfort zone
Has little time for them;
We go our way as if alone;
And pass their requiem.
"Are we their keeper?" we might ask,
"Their suff'ring's not from us.
Our lives already are a task
And cares *our* angelus."

Our mere five thousand steps of pain,
Now plead *their* message clear;
To ease the anguish they sustain
And be their source of cheer.
As long as breath is on our lips,
Some other's woe is more;
Our faith, our care, our stewardship's
Their hope ...
Our heaven's door.

Legacy

I heard a song that touched the heart,
I saw a structure might'ly built,
Such great achievements set apart,
Humbly did my spirit wilt ...
No legacy, no work so grand,
To mark my presence here -
Little left than grain of sand,
Or wispful word I fear.

No mem'ry left -- small wisdom shared,
Outliving me a day,
Though I had wished some might have cared
To say I'd been this way.
Where is it life has taken me?
What can I say I've done?
My mind in clouded memory
Sees little value won.

And so, too soon I'll take my leave,
So sadly do I rue,
Wondering what I did achieve,
Knowing what I knew.
What pain relieved? What hope renewed?
What inspiration wrought?
What lifted soul? What grace imbued?
What useful lessons taught?

Oh Lord, you know what might have been,
Had you prevailed -- not me,
If I had been less selfish then,
And lived more sensibly.
Too late it is those wrongs to right,
The past is set in stone,
And yet ... tomorrow's hopeful light ...
A chance left to atone.

Love's kind forbearance sets me free,
To face the final day,
My guide is true humility,
Forgiveness -- Love's own way.
Although I've fallen short some length,
What should have been my measure,
What matters is Love's lasting strength,
And those who are my treasure.

They are my living legacy,
They'll be so kind to tell,
"A trusted friend to us was he,
We knew and loved him well."

Sirach 44: 1-15

Smiles

The world turns on smiles.
They open doors to other people's hearts,
They are warmth.
They light up eyes and dispense with gloom.
They make friends quickly and engender other smiles to join them.
They melt the ice when people act cold or when they hurt.
They break the gloom when life is hard and sad and frightening.
People spend fortunes and travel far to find them.
Half of entertainment is dedicated to them.
Certain people are sought because of the smiles they bring.
Most jobs are obtained with a smile
... kept with a smile
... enhanced with a smile.
Most sweethearts are courted with a smile.
... won with a smile
... cherished with a smile.
All relationships are affirmed with a smile.
Smiles enliven the past and the present and welcome the future .
They bring back memories of good times past.
They lubricate time.
An hour with many smiles passes quickly.
A day with many smiles is a good day ...
makes the night easier ...
and gives hope for the next day ...
A year with many smiles is the doorway to a happy life.
A lifetime with many smiles is a successful life ...
and a happy life ...
and a life with many friends.
Smiles say a bad situation is now okay.
They invite people who are quiet to speak.
They challenge anger and pain and conceit and all manner of evil.
They are like flashlights -- they bring light to darkness.

Smiles are a major part of the language of friendship.
They are found all over the world and know no boundaries.
They speak all languages.
They are found among people of all ages.
Smiles cost nothing but give everything.
They are what most people want and all people need.
They are found with patience and they quell violence.
They are found with kindness and they sweeten bitterness.
They are found with hope and they lighten despair.
They are honest and genuine and, when faked, do not work.

All the wrinkles of age cannot hide a smile.
They are present in the last moments.
They are always welcome.
Smiles rival the sun, fresh air and warm breezes as a favorite thing.
A smile can be wiped off a face but never erased from a heart.
They like to come back again and again.

They make us feel good, look good, and seek good.
They say, "Hello!"
They say, "Welcome!"
They say, "It's nice to see you!"
They say, "You're okay!"
So smile at your blessings,
Smile through your trials,
Smile with all people,
Smile with your Creator.
See the smiles.
They are everywhere.
They are everything.
They are part of heaven here on earth.

Voices

A dark voice from Sheol said, "Don't do it.
Let better men prevail and don't commit.
You *are* inferior,
They *far* superior ...
Why take a chance on this;
You risk your happiness;
So rest awhile and on your laurels sit."

I thought, "Am I that bad? ... I think I'm not.
At least I should give it a healthy shot,
Those demons spew disgust,
But God espouses trust.
What do I lose when I
Turn heart and hand to try?
If nothing's what I do, I've lost a lot."

"So take the chance though efforts fall and fail.
Good time with full endeavor shall prevail.
Though some, the work debase,
The goodly will embrace.
If done to seek what's true,
I'll find my Xanadu,
And God and inner spirit I'll regale."

So voices you must understand me clear ...
It's truth within the soul that I hold dear.
When we our brother lift
With Spirit's inner gift,
It's Power giving life,
And Truth like surgeon's knife
That cuts through pain and calms the lonely fear!

truths and
omens

Minerva

Amidst the seven hills of passing Rome,
On temple marbles prey to time and wear,
A still Minerva, speaks her pagan truths,
Now passed unseen by choking traffic blur.
Green mold and ice and now the acid rain,
Stick to her crystal frame once loved by all.
Comes hungered dog or ghostly wind to howl,
To join the few within her columned hall.
Bye bye to cultured lands of many gods,
We wiser, now ignore *one* deity,
And sing our hymn to concrete, gold and lust;
A spooky overture to tyranny.

A Sonnet To Time

Like Mercury's course passing in such haste,
Unnoticed but secure its ebb and flow,
Though memory recalls dark nights too slow,
A boy to aged man is quickly traced.
Late brought to live in modern world so paced
That cadenced nature would not pleasure show,
Its beauty lost where wasted chances go,
When life in such swift current is encased.
Too oft were life's gold nuggets lost or spurned,
Whilst speeding time like hungry falcon flew,
Too seldom aged wisdoms fully learned,
Self-choking limits clouding larger view ...
Ticking, ticking ... precious time ... spent fire burned,
Ending, ending ... precious life ... fleet years too few!

Sad and Damning!

Sad and damning the path they trod
With hedonism as their god,
When children pampered fail to grow.
With thankless character they show
That fragile faith is held roughshod
And gold is their divining rod.
A logic that one deems as odd,
When creed espoused is quid pro quo.
Sad and damning!

Would think to mason lowly hod,
Respect would have as grass to sod,
Their Maker held in awe ... but no.
Too filled are they with cold ego,
And so they to the devil nod.
Sad and damning!

Is this to be our nation's lot,
That we our foundings have forgot?
Has nation built on blood and toil,
And sacrifice for freedom's soil,
Lost faith and gratitude to God?
What price paid heroes this land we trod.
Sad and damning!

Dust

The king; the celebrity;
The egoist; the athlete;
The talking head; the yachtsman;
The senator; the anchorman;
The beauty queen; the lottery winner ...
Soon passed away,
And in time,
No one cared that they were gone;
And few remembered ...
As life went on.

A Gifted Hand

Technology enables
Artistry ennobles
A gifted hand.

A gifted hand
Enables technology,
Ennobles artistry.

Y2K Preamble

I woke upon a sunny, sandy shore.
'Twas April now ... fresh scent at winter's door.
A Saturday with birds ... all seemed so dear.
Two thousand was the name of this new year.
I pinched myself a mark ... I still was here.
Blue sky and sand and surf ... what's there to fear?
Look and see. Are there portents to be found?
Wonders in the heavens? Footprints in the ground?
Then ... thunderstruck it came ... a flash of light;
An eerie wakening of sorts that grasps the night ...

A silver awesome glint ... Enola Gay
Banks in the crystal light of early day,
And in a flash ... A dark age lights the sky,
And truth sets thousands free to live ... and die!
Another place another truth to see;
The entrance sign proclaims "Work sets you free"...
They came to test the cleansing of their souls,
And added millions more to prior tolls.
Not since the dawn of time had this prevailed;
Not since man came to be, death so regaled.

More war and killing done these sixty years ...
More earthly damage wreaked ... more pain ... more tears.
So look within, you vain and senseless eyes,
To find the faith once held ... you now despise.
With belly full and greed to mark the path,
You act surprised to see God's awful wrath.
Sixty turns around the sun ... That's the sign.
A world once beautiful in life benign,
Now pained and troubled ... torn and restless sphere.
Its path awry with err ... and whom to steer?

Speak of hope -- but by God you better know,
Sure omen are the seeds of death you sow.
Vile death ... corroded, stocked and seeping slime.
Buried places ... saved dark for future time.
Shameful and secret caves of world and mind.
Violence craved and bred ... a world gone blind.
We legislate our lies, ignoring truth;
Abandon and abuse our gifted youth;
Indifferent to their pleas, we teach them naught,
And watch in horror, struck at what is wrought!

The prophets here and there are painting black,
An ebony of thought ... left ... right ... and back.
"Rain forests burned and hacked to desert waste.
The virtued guides to life *crack*ed and debased.
The seven deadly sins release their fumes
To find and send our babes to early tombs.
Empty hearts scorned and teaching empty hearts;
Abandoned children left as hope departs ...
Steered on to faint but certain course of doom
Because the world gives love the smallest room."

Our Mother Earth bleeds life from every pore
To spill and be defiled in hate and war.
We must pause ... *now* ... to bind and heal these things,
Restoring love and all the hope it brings.
Blue marble of the earth ... gem of the sky ...
Creation's gift for man to sanctify
With amity and equity to share,
With unity and charity and care.
Millennium has come with signs and choice ...
Pursue the course of doom ... or hear Love's voice!

Invisible

"That squalid, repulsive creature;
Clumsy, awkward, homely bastard",
They called him,
"What has he that anyone would turn and seek?"
Ugly, living curse of a man;
Who looks at all and wanes
Into a small vial of nothingness,
And soon withers
In the beauty of it all.

Invisible

With no one caring ...

An Empty Room

The room is empty now ... 'tis still ... indeed.
Whatever goodness dwelt within these walls?
Or heartened touch that eased a pain ... or soothed its calls?
What vestige lies within this room that one should heed?
The room is empty now ... what can it tell?

The room is simple ... sure enough ... and low,
A place a thousand others surely would agree
Is theirs ... and yet there seems to be
A soul within ... though dimly felt ... a humble glow ...
The room is empty now ... a quiet shell.

There isn't book or note or telling artifact
That gives a hint of who the tenant be,
Or how a life was lived or of its final plea,
Or how its soul was rich or what it lacked ...
The room is empty now ... a lonely cell.

A life was lived here once ... now little known ...
Where is the family? Where is the friend?
Where is the liveliness? Why did it end?
A soul unique ... or made another's clone?
The room is empty now ... with musty smell.

What if the room were yours ... and you not there?
What would these walls reveal to sing your song?
Would any feel compelled to stay here long?
To say a prayer for you ... or even care?
The room is empty now ... what does it tell?

Addressing The Gifted

How blessed are the gifts you so display;
A power only God could deign to share ...
With measure great and substance sweet and fair
You open heaven's light to blackened day.
A magic has within you built such charms ...
A singular and brightly shining glow ...
A beacon given we who live below ...
That catches short, surprises and disarms ...
Let trueness flow, let brilliance show,
"Bravo!" say we, "Bravo! Bravo! Bravo!"

How can you with such majesty employ
Pure elements of thought expressed so true?
Did prior life give genius you pulled through?
Are you a man or unseen godly toy?
With eager grasp would many others claim
Those blessed gifts and charms so richly yours;
With pretense take as theirs what God assures
To you for you to give ... but in His name.
Let trueness flow, let brilliance show,
"Bravo!" say we, "Bravo! Bravo! Bravo!"

Imposters who would seek another's gold
Or wit or charm or place or brilliant light ...
Would better seek gifts of their own to cite.
Those gifts are there but some are deeply souled;
Found in the heart by prayer and wisdom's toil ...
Outside of self in giving, caring deed ...
In smiles and cheer and sharing practiced creed ...
Not shown in pride but sown in humble soil,
"Bravo!" say we, "Bravo! Bravo! Bravo!"

But we a larger mystic body be
Where *each* is given boundless gifts to give
And joy to share the gifts that others live
Without a want for more ... nor jealousy.
So make your treasure mine for just today
As we in selfless acts our treasures share,
In knowledge that all gifts that we declare
Are God's ... that we in love must give away.
Let trueness flow, let brilliance show,
"Bravo!" say we, "Bravo! Bravo! Bravo!"

Romans 12: 4-31

Early Riser

In early morn before the sun,
Well nigh before the coffee's done,
A restless thought shook me awake;
I rose disturbed my day to make.
Lying in that prone position,
Mind's eye in sullen recognition,
Saw new-born babe there in wee bed,
Saw old man weak with heavy head.
Each lay there horizontally,
And hardly stirred with energy,
And in that vision in my mind,
I gained a liveliness to find ...
That lying in that morning sleep,
Prevented me my goals to keep,
So I came forth to greet the dawn
With spirit, hope and gritty yawn.
So much of life is in the prone,
That even rising there alone,
Was better than those lengthy sleeps
Because too soon we're there for keeps!

Remember

O, to remember each time been and done,
When Creation,
In vast and myriad beauties
Permeated my small and humble soul
And caused it to become silent;
That true and only prayer it could offer ...

There I stand ... unable to express
Anything to or of the Majesty the envelopes me;
Overwhelms me ...
That ubiquitous power of beauty and love
Speaks to me at my very center ...
In silence ... and awe.

In the mists of human torpor
Where I reside,
Light shines upon the dark-scaled eyes within
And opens them to wonder.
Then something beyond description
Enters my soul ...

******

*"Remember what you have seen
because everything forgotten
returns to the circling winds."*
Navajo chant

From The Heart

We strive to find that golden soul within;
Rare sanctum of those dreams of truth and light;
Inspired words so deep below the skin;
The stuff of beauty touched ... and framed just right.
In this comes mystic path from soul to soul,
Not hampered by the spoken masks of men;
Good seed to find their once-held inner call.

Perhaps in this, there really are no rules;
Or maybe it is we, mere knaves and fools;
E'er trying new attempts to turn their mind
To greater Spirit's call and truth to find;
Rhyme may not matter; structure less in vogue ...
Yea ... just speak songs they'll treasure with your brogue!

Biography

Rich Houseknecht was born in Batavia, New York, in 1931, the youngest of five sons of Seward and Kathryn Houseknecht. After serving with the 25th Infantry Division in Korea in 1951-52, he completed studies for degrees in engineering and education and worked in those fields until his retirement in 1991. He now works as a volunteer in his church and community, serving in various capacities with organizations dedicated to assisting poor and disadvantaged persons, most recently with the homeless.

Mr. Houseknecht has written poetry for a number of years but only recently considered publishing his work to leave as a legacy to his children and grandchildren. When he decided to share his poetry on a wider scale, it was well received.. Several of his poems have been published including, To My Grandchild, Minerva, Late Autumn, A Lad at Bedtime and A Wooded Pond At Twilight, the latter given the Editor's Choice Award by The Poetry Guild for its 1998 International Poetry Competition.